Learning 07

怎樣寫好英文作文

應 用 進 階 篇

吳奚真／主編

張先信 · **Phillip Podgur**／編著

序

　　英語教學要培養四種基本能力：聽的能力、閱讀能力、口頭表達能力和文字表達能力。正常的英語教學，應該發揮這四種功能。在考試領導教學的情形下，對於中學生英文寫作能力的培養，荒廢已久，現在大專聯考加考英文作文，將有助於英文教學的正常化，充分實現這門課程的多元目標。在這一方面，我想最重要的是按照正常程序教學，不必有什麼大更張，很自然而輕鬆地培養起學生的英文文字表達能力，不要剛從一種偏差回過頭來，又鑽進一個新的牛角尖。

　　一項學習活動，要由希望獲得的成果來決定。英文的口頭表達能力和筆寫表達能力，各有其不同的培養途徑。就筆寫表達能力而言，最根本的辦法當然是從培養語言習慣做起，很自然地養成基本的表達能力。但是在目前我國英語教學的客觀條件之下，似乎還不容易很圓滿地做到這一點。而且口說的語言和筆寫的文字之間總是有些距離的。一種外國語的學習，本來就是一個記憶和模仿的過程，不論是有意的，還是無意的。口語如此，文字的表達亦然。在文字的表達方面，需要更為嚴密的組織和正確無訛的形式，就是要字斟句酌；這種能力的培養，就我國中學生而言，更有賴於有意的記憶和模仿。

　　要想寫出清通的合乎習慣用法的英文，至少要熟讀若干篇適當的文章，融會貫通，熟諳基本的句法和常用的成語，到作文的時候才能做靈活的運用，正確而有效地表達出自己的意思。把這個基礎打好，可以終身受用。事實上，中學的英文課本裡面的文章應該是很好的模仿對象，不過有些教材可能與現實生活環境有些距離，或文體比較老式，因而效果不彰。老一輩的人從前在小學和初中時代要學作文言文。怎樣才能作文言文呢？不二的法門就是先熟讀若干篇文章，如《飲冰室文集》之類作品，爛熟胸中，自然就能下筆自如。現在中學生作英文作文，頗有類於從前小學生學作文言文。要熟讀範文，才會作文。當然每次背誦的份量不能太多，以免構成學生的過重負荷，產生不良作用。

　　本書的編著，就是希望能就英文作文提供一種比較實用的教材或讀物，以求達成學習的效果。全書分基礎入門篇和應用進階篇，基礎入門篇章討論句子和段落，所提供的例文和例句，都儘量選取文字簡練、難易適度、內容豐富有意義的文字，其中很多可以當作模仿的對象。並附有豐富的練習，使學生得以培養基本的寫作能力。在最後的「總練習」裡，我們提供二十個作文題目，每個題目下面並附有提示，供學生練習寫作八十字左右的短文。應用進階篇討論全篇的英文作文，提供範文二十三篇，有些篇是由編著者撰寫的，有些篇是改寫的，屬於四種不同的體裁，內容採用中國本位，儘量以中學生的現實生活為題材。對字彙和成語加以控制，並使之重複出現，每篇均詳加注釋，對成語用法提供例句。為便利教學並供學生自修起見，範文均附有中文翻譯。每篇後面的練習分為三部分：第一部分是問答，幫助學生嫻熟範文內容。第二部分是中譯英，由學生練習使用本課學過的成語。第三部分是作文。作文的長度請教師斟酌決定，大致可分為三個階段：第一階段每篇以二百字為度，第二階段三百字，第三階段四百字或更多。

　　本書對於作文方法只做概要的敘述，並就每篇範文的結構略作評釋。在這一方面，學生只要能達到最基本的要求就好了。中學生在中文作文方面已有相當的經驗；就文章做法而言，中文和英文是一樣的。在目前這個階段，最重要的是訓練學生寫出通順英文的能力，進一步的寫作技巧，不妨留待大學裡面的英文作文課程來培養。

　　張先信教授在國立臺灣師範大學英語系講授英文作文多年，在這方面具有豐富的經驗。師大英語系美籍講師白非力先生（Phillip Podgur）　本書備有習題解答，供參考之用。

　　本書於編著及校訂過程中雖極審慎，疏漏之處仍屬難免，尚希方家惠予指正。

　　　　　　　　　　　　　　　　　　　　吳奚眞

目　　錄

第一章 作文的形式

一篇形式完整的英文作文至少要有三段：第一段叫做開頭段落（the beginning paragraph），第二段叫做中間段落（the middle paragraph），最後一段叫做結尾段落（the ending paragraph）。在我們討論這三種段落的寫法之前，請先閱讀下面這篇文章。

Killing for Sport Is Pure Evil

To me it is unimaginable how anyone could think an animal more interesting dead than alive. I can also easily prove to my own satisfaction that killing "for sport" is the perfect type of pure evil for which philosophers have sometimes sought.

Most wicked deeds are done because the doer seeks some good for himself. The liar lies to gain some end; the swindler and the thief want things which, if honestly obtained, might be good in themselves. Even the murderer may be removing an obstacle to normal desires or gaining possession of something which his victim keeps from him. None of these people usually does evil for evil's sake. They are selfish or dishonest, but their deeds are not

necessarily evil. The killer for sport has no such understandable motive. He prefers death to life, darkness to light. He gets nothing except the satisfaction of saying, "Something which wanted to live is dead. There is that much less vitality, consciousness, and, perhaps, joy in the universe." When a man purposely destroys one of the works of man we call him a vandal. When he purposely destroys one of the works of God we call him a sportsman.

The hunter-for-food may be as wicked and as misguided as vegetarians sometimes say; but he does not kill for the sake of killing. The rancher and the farmer who kill all living things not immediately profitable to them may sometimes harm their own best interests; but whether they do or do not they hope to achieve some supposed good by their killing. If to do evil not in the hope of gain but for evil's sake involves the greatest wrong man can do, then killing for killing's sake is a terrifying phenomenon and as strong a proof as we could have of that "reality of evil" with which present-day Philosophers are again concerned.

　　上面這篇文章一共有三段，作者在本文中反覆討論一個主題：
「為娛樂而殺生」是十足的罪惡。

　　第一段為引言（introduction）。這是一篇短文，所以引言也很
短，一共只有兩句。作者在本段中簡潔地指出了他將在本文中討論的
主題。

　　第二段為主體（the body）。作者在本段中提出各種事實，反覆討
論，分析「為娛樂而殺生者」的動機。

　　第三段為結尾（the ending）。作者在本段中繼續比較分析，最後
作結論，說明「為娛樂而殺生」的確是一種十足的罪惡。

　　本文的特色是，形式完整、結構嚴謹，作者提出各種事實，反覆
討論，證明他的論點是正確的。這是一篇很好的議論文。

第一節　開頭段落

在一篇作文的開頭,你是第一次跟讀者接觸。你要是已經擬妥中間段落的大綱,就等於是已經計劃好討論主題的中心思想。因此你眼前要做的並不是你準備說什麼,而是怎麼樣開始。你想給讀者一個好印象,讓他一看到你的作文立刻就會感到興趣,而且急著要往下看。為了要達到這個目的,你必須盡一切努力,使作文的開頭具有極大的吸引力。

好的開頭段落並不是偶然的,也不是靠耍花招能收效的,必須經過深思熟慮妥善設計,以便和其餘的段落筆調一致。你要是想以輕鬆、幽默的筆調來寫整篇作文,就必須用同樣的筆調來寫開頭的引言。你要是想提出嚴肅的論點,從第一個字開始就得讓讀者感到嚴肅。

然而,寫作文開頭段落的方法並非是一成不變的,要視題目、內容的性質以及寫作的方法而定。學作文的人應該熟習下面這些寫開頭段落的方法,以便實地寫作時能作適當的選擇。

Ⅰ．敘述 (Narrative)

有經驗的作家多以敘述的方式來開始一篇文章,以引起讀者的興趣。同樣的,你也可以用這種方式來開始一篇作文。你可以談自己的親身經歷,也可以談父母或親友的經歷,也可以談報章雜誌或書裡提到的故事。不過,千萬要注意,用來開始一篇作文的故事,一定要跟討論的中心思想有關係;故事的細節要恰到好處,不能拖得太長,因

為引言只是整個作文的一小部分。

現在請讀下面一個開頭段落，這是一篇以 Just a Card 為題目的作文的開頭一段，描寫一份成績單上的某項分數使一個學生感到痛苦的情形：

> He just sat there, motionless, too stunned to
> speak. His head ached, and wild, improbable
> thoughts ran through his brain. How could she have
> done this to him?

上面這個開頭段落便是以敘述的方式寫成的，十分簡短，但很有力。

II. 開門見山 （Direct）

對學寫作文的人來說，用開門見山的方式來開始一篇作文比較穩妥。你可以直截了當地告訴讀者你將在這篇作文裡討論什麼，從而引導他的思想方向。用這種方式來寫開頭的段落比較容易。

現在請讀下面一個開頭段落，這是一篇以 Part Time Jobs 為題目的作文的頭一段：

> Recently, when I found I had some extra time
> on my hands, I went out and got myself a part time
> job. I can truthfully say I'm glad I did. What's it
> like? Why do I enjoy it? Let me tell you.

上面這個開頭段落便是以開門見山的方式寫成的。第一句就指出了全文的主題；兩個問句使這篇作文富有口語的語調，並且暗示出中間段落要寫些什麼。

III. 談細節 （Detailed）

儘管事實、統計數位、引用語或其他的具體資料用在中間段落最有效，這種細節照樣可以用在一篇作文的開頭段落中，以引起人們的注意。用細節來開始一篇作文，可以使中心思想顯得更權威，使讀者對你的意見和結論信服。但是，務必要牢記在心，引言只能暗示，不能明示。不要在頭一段裡浪費太多重要的資料，以免在其餘的段落裡一再重覆此種資料。

現在請讀下面一個開頭段落，這是一篇以 Nature's Water Cycle 為題目的文章的頭一段：

> Only a bout 3 per cent of the water on earth is fresh water—and most of it is not easily available to man. It includes water locked in glaciers and icecaps, more than 2 per cent of the earth's water. About half of 1 per cent of the earth's water is beneath the earth's surface. Rivers and lakes contain only about one-fiftieth of 1 per cent of the earth's water.

上面這個開頭段落便是以談細節的方式寫成的。第一句便用一個統計數字指出地球上淡水的數量，其餘三句也用約略的數字暗示出淡水分布的情形。讀者看過這樣一個開頭段落以後，自然想知道更多的細節，繼續往下看。

IV. 描寫 (Descriptive)

　　有的時候，生動的背景能使你所要表達的主要意思更為突出、更為清晰。所以，你可以用描寫的方式，在讀者心中創造一幅生動的圖畫，使他在不知不覺中進入你要討論的範圍。譬如說，你打算討論消除貧民區或校園中有礙觀瞻的事物，你不妨在開頭一段中詳細描寫一番，然後再提出你的論點或建議。

　　現在請讀下面一個開頭段落，這是一篇以God's World為題目的作文的頭一段：

> You look up at the sky. The black clouds have blown out the sun's golden rays. The soft warm wind has become cold and fierce. Trees that gently swayed in the faint breeze now unwillingly bow their heads to a mighty unseen master. The wind is howling out its anger.

上面這個開頭段落便是用描寫的方式寫成的。這段對雲彩、氣溫和風勢的描寫，在讀者心中創造了一幅暴風雨即將來臨的圖畫。

第二節　中間段落

　　中間段落為整篇作文的主體,少則一段,多則數段。作者應在中間段落中列舉重要事實及細節,以闡釋引言中所提示的主題或中心思想。中間段落不但要上承引言,下啟結論,而且要前後呼應,脈絡一貫。

　　現在請閱讀這篇作文:

True　Friendship

　　Throughout my life my pets have been a great help to me and a wonderful pleasure. Animals have also been some of my truest friends.

　　My dog, Wolf, was the first firend I ever had. When I was three years old my father came home one night with a large box which contained a German police dog. Wolf seemed to understand me better than my mother or father. We lived in the country so there was no one but the dog to look after me. As I grew older, Wolf and I spent many happy days playing together. He even pulled my wagon when I played farmer. My mother never had to worry about my eating for Wolf wouldn't let me leave the table until I had eaten all that had been

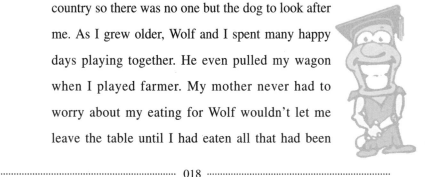

given to me. When I was seven we moved to Texas and the dog was left with some neighbors.

Triangle was a horse that was owned by the man on the next ranch. Everyday after shool I would run to the fields where he would be eating. After a few months we became the best of friends and Triangle let me ride him. One day I saw my father talking to Mr. Aston, our neighbor and also the owner of my new friend. They called to me and I advanced with some fear. Mr. Aston had seen me ride Triangle and he was telling my father that I was mounting a wild horse that had never been trained. I was quite shocked but I didn't let the men know. My father died shortly after, and we moved again. Triangle was left in Texas.

Since we now lived in a city and I don't think it is fair to lock up animals, I got myself a fish tank. There was no greater pleasure for me than to watch for hours the different types of fish on the other side of the glass. It was almost as if I had a window that looked into another world. As school became more important to me I had less time for my fish and so my mother took care to them.

It is a wonderful feeling to have a warm friend waiting for you when you get home. It matters little whether it is a dog, cat, or even a monkey. I hope everyone can have the pleasure from pets that I have had.

上面這篇作文一共有五段，主要是敘述作者如何與他的寵物建立起親密的友誼。

第一段為開頭段落，也是本文的引言。作者在這一段中簡潔地指出全文的主題：在他的一生當中，寵物給了他很大的助益和快樂，動物也成了他真正的朋友。

第二段至第四段皆為中間段落，也是本文的主體。作者在這三段中舉出具體事實，說明如何與他的寵物建立起真正的友誼。第二段主要是敘述一條德國警犬 Wolf 如何成為作者的第一個朋友；第三段主要是敘述一匹紅棕色種馬Triangle如何與作者成為好朋友；第四段主要是敘述一缸觀賞魚給予他多麼大的快樂。這三段雖然各自獨立，界限分明，但前後呼應，脈絡一貫，因為各段所討論的都是作者所喜愛的寵物。

第五段結尾段落，也是本文的結論。作者在這一段中作了一個簡單的結論，他指出有位熱誠的朋友等著你回家該是一種多麼奇妙的感受，希望大家都能享有這種快樂。

本文的特色是，形式完整、文字平實，作者並將各種動物「擬人化」（personalizing），使他和寵物之間的關係顯得格外親密。

第三節　結尾段落

寫結尾段落時，千萬不要用 "In conclusion…" 或 "To sum up…" 之類的套語，否則會顯得呆板、沉悶。也不能突然終止，使讀者產生言有未盡之感。因此，在討論怎樣寫好的結尾段落之前，我們特別要在這裡指出結尾的六戒：

1. 戒用一個簡短的句子結尾。即使是職業作家也很難用一個簡短的句子來結尾，初學寫作的人更不能用這種方式來寫結尾段落。

2. 戒重覆。已經在中間段落中討論過的論點，不要再在結尾段落中重覆。

3. 戒空洞。不要在結尾段落中寫出沒有內容，沒有意義的句子，否則會令讀者大失所望的。

4. 戒離題。結尾段落應就中間段落所討論的中心思想作一總結，不能扯到別的主題去，不然就會產生混亂，使讀者摸不著頭腦。

5. 戒令人生厭或自作聰明。在敘述進入高潮時，切勿節外生枝，使讀者感到厭煩。

6. 戒用浮詞或意象。在結尾段落中忌用浮誇的詞句或意象，否則你自己會不知所云，讀者也會莫名其妙。

一個好的結尾段落應該直截了當、長短適中、不呆板、不沉悶、不做作。首先要根據選擇的題目、討論的中心思想和寫作的方法，確定結尾段落的形式，然後順理成章、自然而且有力地做出結論。今將

寫作結尾段落常用的技巧舉例說明如下：

I． 敘述 （Narrative）

　　像引言一樣，結尾段落也可以用敘述的方式來寫。用這種方式來結尾，可收令人驚奇的效果。下面便是一篇以The Punk（不良少年）為題目的作文的結尾段落。該文的大意是：一天夜晚，有個不良少年夥同幫中其他的份子出外尋樂，把別人的輪胎割破。他回家發現父親心臟病發作，但醫生遲遲未到。以下便是這篇作文的結尾段落：

> The doctor looked at him sadly "Is that what you think, son？ I'm sorry that you do. It's just that some punks slit my tires on Thirty-fifth Street, and I was delayed getting here. I didn't kill you father, son. They did."

II． 提示 （Suggestive）

　　作者可就中間段落所討論的問題，在結尾段落中提示一套解決的辦法。下面便是一篇以Political Indifference（對政治漠不關心）為題目的文章的結尾段落。該文的大意是：一般美國公民對於地方、全國和世界的事情並無適當的了解，作者對於這種情形加以責難，然後舉出這種持續的淡漠態度對於自由可能造成的危害。他在結論中提示一些解決的辦法：

> What this country needs is some preventive medicine. There should be more public information

releases by the government on the state of the union. Debates between opposite parties should be held on television, during the evening hours, so that adults could watch and be informed. People should be encouraged to write to their congressmen and keep themselves in touch with what is going on in Washington. If these and other similar measures were followed, I believe the shameful title of this essay would find its way only into the pages of the history books.

III. 畫龍點睛 （Focused）

作者先在前面各段中作廣泛的描述，然後在結尾段落中以畫龍點睛的手法明示全文的主旨或本意。下面便是一篇以My Dream House（我夢想的住宅）為題目的作文的結尾段落。該文的大意是：作者描述她有一天能擁有一座巨大的住宅，裡面滿是最新式的設備，然後在最後一段中明白指出她這個夢的本意：

Altogether I expect my dream house to have twenty-two rooms, no more, no less. If you start to count you will find that I plan to have sixteen bedrooms. This will be a necessity for I also will have seventeen children, all girls, who will be well-trained in the art of maintaining a home of this size.

IV. 預期 (Prediction)

　　你在中間段落裡談過你的觀點之後，可以在結尾段落中談談你對將來的期望。像這樣，可使讀者對你的觀點有進一步的了解，並加強全文的中心意思。下面便是一篇以 Park in Winter（冬天的公園）為題目的作文的結尾段落：

> I may see the park today and forget it. Months from now, when the trees' arms are full, and the earth has regrown its hair, and the flowers smell of sweet nature, and bird hum silly tunes, and people have awakened this sleeping thing—I will recall the park in winter.

V. 比較 (Comparison or Contrast)

　　假如你寫的是很久以前發生的事情，你可以在結尾段落中就過去和現在的差異作個簡短的比較。下面是一位匈牙利難民以 Memories of Home（念故鄉）為題所寫的作文的結尾段落：

> Eight months ago, when I arrived in America, I again found my blue sky. It is brighter, bluer, clearer than over my country. I hope, I wish, that some day the sky over my country will be bright, too.

練　習　一

I. 下面各開頭段落係用下面四種技巧當中的一種寫成的，在各段下面的空白內填入該段所用技巧的名稱。

> Narrative
>
> Direct
>
> Detailed
>
> Descriptive

A.　While resting the other day, I sat down to figure out just how much time I've spent talking on our "Today" show since it went on the air in 1952 .The astonishing answer was—roughly 1700 hours! At an average speaking rate, that comes to more than 12 million words—enough to fill more than 120 full-length books!

_____

B.　The night air calls to you from the broken pane of glass in the window. You walk over and stare out into the chill of December. Your ears tell you that the night is screaming for you to come. The hall closet door opens; you grab your coat and walk out into the loneliness of the night. The biting wind stabs through you. You start to walk and the echo of your footsteps makes a disordered pattern like the years of your life.

_____

C. What do parents (a species which is considered outdated by the younger generation) think about teenagers going steady? Well, I hear about it plenty······ from my dad.

_____

D. In the peace and quiet of surrounding hemlock he rests. To the West, in the valley, the river where he swam in his youth goes to sea. Upon the hill is the house, the beginning of his journey and the end. Towering elms look tenderly upon the beautiful building. The lawn green flows over the earth. The oak with limbs heavy with age shelters the soft sadness with its broad leaves. And the sky, a heavenly roof, rains its peace on this place, the place where a man found rest from the stress of a devoted life.

_____

II. 下面各結尾段落係用下面五種技巧當中的一種寫成的，在各段下面的空白內填入該段所用技巧的名稱。

> Narrative
>
> Suggestive
>
> Prediction
>
> Comparison or Contrast

A. Last but not least, the good guest knows when to leave a party. Keep an eye on the clock (it's an unwise hostess who doesn't have one in

view) and go when it tells you to go. Tell your hostess how much you have enjoyed her party—and be gone.

B. The lean and slender horseman, dressed in black, passed quickly out of sight. He did not look back. Alone and standing upright in the forest clearing was a small tombstone, with the epitaph that said simply:

Born 1816   Died 1837

Beloved by All

Ann Rutledge

C. Sandys lacks his father-in-law's skill at speaking, but otherwise there are many similarities ——the delight in working all night, the youthful rebelliousness, the utter certainty of the expert amateur. In the end, sheer competence and fierce determination may make him the Queen's first minister. If this should happen, few people, and certainly not Duncan Sandys, would be surprised.

D. The stakes are high for all of us. But if we are successful, if the railroads are made of stronger and lighter materials, as I am confident they can be, they will perform their mass-transportation function more cheaply

and more efficiently than has ever been known before. I see an industry that will be continuing to pay—not spend—tax dollars. Finally, I see an industry growing in volume, increasing its employment and growing in the service that it renders to the public.

Ⅲ. 在下面一篇文章中，原來分開的段落已被合併成一段，在應該另起一段的第一個字下面畫一條底線。

  I can never forget the day I went swimming during the month of March. The sky was blue but the temperature was a chilly 10 degrees centigrade. I am not in the habit of doing this but was tricked into it. Some friends had said I would not have the nerve to go swimming at that time of the year. Not wanting to be called a coward. I had accepted their dare. My friends and I piled into a car and drove to the beach after lunch. We arrived there at about two o'clock in the afternoon. Five minutes later I had changed into my swimming attire, which consisted of an outfit worn by Navy frogmen. I ran into the water and remained in the pounding surf less time than it took me to dress. The ocean, I might add, was a bit cool, but I didn't mind it. My outfit was insulated for just this type of weather. After I came

out of the water, I quickly ran into my car which was parked nearby and changed into some warm clothing. That evening I began to feel a little cold coming on. I called my doctor and told him the story. He prescribed some special pills that cost a dollar each. I was to remain in bed and take one of these pills every hour for twenty-four hours. One hour I was to take a pink pill, another hour a green pill, changing the procedure every four hours. After taking enough pills to feel I was loaded with buckshot, I recovered without any harmful results. Here is a word of wisdom to anyone who is thinking of going swimming in the month of March. Don't ! You may enjoy taking pills, however. I know I don't.

第二章　四種文體

按照體裁來分，文章大致可以分為四種：描寫文（Descriptive Essays），說明文（Expository Essays），記敘文（Narrative Essays），議論文（Argumentative Essays）。

第一節　描寫文

描寫文的內容主要是描寫，雖然其中免不了會有相當數量的敘述。描寫的對象可以是一個景象、風景、建築物、人、動物、或一系列的事情（如一場球類比賽）等。

描寫文的主要目的，是把作者心中的一幅圖畫，很清晰而確切地轉移到讀者的心中。就此點而言，描寫文類似一幅素描或速寫。速寫要把所有的要點和許多細節畫出來，使看的人對於所描繪的東西得到一個正確、真實而生動的印象。速寫不是照片，也不是藍圖，所以若干細節和實際的尺寸或面積都可以略去。但是大致的輪廓和大小要表現出來，使看的人得到一個正確的整體印象。一篇描寫文如果能像一幅速寫那樣地提供一幅確實可靠的概括性的圖畫，就可以說是圓滿地達成了任務。

現在以範文1. Our Next-Door Neighbors（p.50）為例，說明描寫文的寫法：

第一段以一句諺語 "Good fences make good neighbors" 開頭，以展開對近鄰的描寫。這是一種常用的方式，頗能引起讀者的注意。全

文共有七段,第一段只有一個句子,僅佔兩行多一點,可以說是一段簡短有力的引言。

第二段主要是描寫作者的鄰居喜歡借東西。第一句即為本段的主題句,其餘的句子則舉出若干事實,分別證明隔壁張家一家大小如何喜歡借這借那。本段並引用了部分談話,如 "the milkman forgot us this morning, Mrs. Huang" 及 "to save me from going out today",更增加了描寫的生動。

第三段的第一句為本段的主題句,說明作者的近鄰喜歡製造噪音。本段其餘各句分別指出張家如何在大清早或深夜,尤其是星期天早上,製造各種噪音。

第四段主要是描寫張家凡事都要和黃家比,而且不服氣。第一句為主題句,其餘各句列舉具體事實,描寫張家如何東施效顰,處處模仿黃家。

第五段主要是描寫張家愛針對黃家的缺點發表意見,令人厭惡。

第六段主要是描寫張家的寵物。張家的貓和狗很像他們的主人,不安分,喜歡侵擾黃家。本段末句指出,張家的作風使黃家受盡了活罪。

第七段為本文的結尾段落。作者在本段中作了一個很幽默的結尾:如果他們搬走了,我們會想念他們。

整個說來,這是一篇生動的描寫文。第一段為引言;第七段為結尾;第二至六段為主體,列舉主要事實,證明作者近鄰各種可笑的作風。整篇文章始終圍繞著主題,對近鄰作深入的刻畫,所以這也是一篇形式完整、十分連貫的描寫文。

第二節　說明文

說明文要把一個主題的各個方面加以解說，或提供一項完全的說明，細節比較不重要。說明文會包含一些描寫，但是除了描寫之外，要說明一種事物如何發揮功能，同其他事物的關係，也要提到主題事物的過去情形和未來發展，或就因果關係加以闡釋。

說明文的範圍較廣；凡是不僅僅屬於描寫、記敘、或議論範圍的作文，都可以列入說明文項下。這種文體的功能是向讀者說明某項事物，使讀者了解或信服，或使讀者感動。

現在以範文5. Swimming（p.94）為實例，說明此種文體的寫法：

第一段為引言，主要說明人類必須經過學習才會游泳。

第二段主要說明游泳的重要性。作者列舉事實，說明會游泳不但能救自己的性命，也能救別人的性命。

第三段主要說明怎樣才能學會游泳，那就是要有信心。本段引述了一個墜海漁夫的故事，更增加了這篇文章的趣味和說服力。

第四段為結論，作者在本段中再度強調會游泳的好處，游泳實在值得學習。

這篇文章一共只有四段，卻簡單扼要地說明了游泳的重要性和好處，是篇典型的說明文。

第三節　記敘文

　　記敘文敘述一件或一系列真實的或想像的事情。題材要能使讀者感到興趣，敘述的方式要能抓住讀者的注意力。純粹的記敘文很少見，裡面或多或少總會摻雜一些描寫，但是以記敘為主。

　　開頭很重要。作文的時間有限，你不能寫得太長。所以，開頭的一段應該是簡明而引人入勝的，馬上引導出故事的本身。有經驗的作者可以從故事中間的重要之處講起，然後用倒敘法（flashback）把前面的一部分補敘出來。但是對一個沒有很多經驗的中學生來說，這個辦法有些冒險。

　　中間段落應該只講述和主題有關的事情，不相干的枝節一律摒棄。把主要的事情按照時間先後或主題的順序講述，力求簡潔明白。

　　結尾的一段除了把故事作一結束之外，最好能蘊含一點意義，耐人尋味，或使讀者有所領悟。

　　記敘文的應用很廣，可用來敘述發生在我們周遭的一切事物，也可以用來寫書信、日記、新聞報導、歷史、自傳及傳記，大部分的小說也都是用記敘文寫成的。

　　現以範文17. Typhoon（p.196）為例，說明記敘文的寫法：

　　第一段為引言，敘述颱風貝蒂將襲擊臺北的消息。

　　第二段敘述作者全家如何立刻作好防颱準備，連他們家的北京狗「小白」也跑來跑去，偶爾發出吠聲，平添不少緊張的氣氛。

　　第三段敘述颱風來襲時大家正在吃晚飯，電燈也突然滅了，情況越來越緊張。

　　第四段敘述父子倆點蠟燭的經過，父親的一句話 "That's okay, son," 使這段敘述顯得更為生動，也增加了全家人的安全感。

　　第五段敘述全家繼續吃晚飯的情形，這時屋子外面已是風狂雨驟。

　　第六段敘述另一個緊張的局面，「小白」自風雨中從後門奔入屋子，給大家帶來一場虛驚。

　　第七、八兩段敘述颱風襲擊的高潮，風勢強烈，作者家裡的一棵木瓜樹連根拔起。但父親沉著的話語使大家稍微安心一點。

　　第九段為結尾段落，敘述貝蒂颱風襲擊過後的災情。

　　這篇記敘文按照時間先後的順序，敘述貝蒂颱風來襲的緊張氣氛，其間高潮迭起，偶爾穿插一句對話，使敘述益顯生動，緊張中略見輕鬆。此種文體的敘述易流於枯燥單調，但本文並沒有這種情形。

第四節　議論文

議論文是就引起大家爭論的一個主題，表明你個人的意見，目的是要說服那些想法和你不同的人，使他們接受你的意見。

為了達到這個目的，議論文的文字必須清晰有力，論點必須合理中肯，並且要用充分的理由來支持自己的論點，使之具有說服力。

通常可以把所要駁斥的論點放在開頭，然後逐步提出自己的論點。把最有力的論點放在最後，那樣可以發揮更大的效果。

在議論文裡面，要避免使用純然感情用事的字句。

現在以範文 22. Is Television Harmful to Children? （p.242）為例，說明議論文的寫法：

第一段為引言，指出電視對兒童的影響好壞都有，而且壞的影響居多。

第二段指出電視的好處，把電視比做百科全書，一個兒童在客廳裡看一個小時教育性節目所得的收穫，比在圖書館待一天所得到的還要多。

第三段談的也是電視的好處，電視可以激發兒童豐富的想像力。

第四段則指出電視的不良影響，兒童易於模仿卡通片裡的暴力行為。

第五段是指出做父母的如何濫用電視節目來安撫子女，讓他們受到暴力卡通和道德淪喪的連續劇的不良影響。

第六段是指出快步調的電視節目容易使兒童變得沒有耐心，不用頭腦。

　　第七段為結論，指出電視的確對兒童有很大影響，造成許多急待解決的問題。

　　這是一篇典型的議論文，反覆辯論電視對兒童的影響，作者始終強調自己所持的觀點，明白指出電視對兒童弊多於利。

第三章　怎樣寫出好的作文

　　作文的基本原則，是必須針對主題發揮，按照適當的順序安排各項資料，前後呼應，層次分明。文字方面，則應力求簡明清晰。一篇好的作文自有其與眾不同之處，不過，凡是好的作文，必定具有下面三種共同的性質：統一性（unity）、連貫性（coherence）和適當的強調（appropriate emphasis）。

第一節　作文的統一性

　　我們已經在基礎入門篇的第四章第一節中討論句子的統一性，在第五章第三節中討論過段落的統一性，現在要討論整篇作文的統一性。段落的統一性，是指一段裡面各個句子的意思必須與該段的中心思想有關係；整篇作文的統一性，則指各段的思想和內容必須與全文的主題有密切關係，一定要絲絲入扣，凡是不相干的枝節，不必要或無意義的字句，都應該一律摒棄，絕對不作毫無關聯或漫無邊際的敘述。比方說，你要是用「台灣的交通」為題寫一篇作文，那你就可以在第一段中概括地指出台灣的交通十分發達；然後在第二段中討論台灣的陸上交通，包括重要的鐵公路系統以及各大城市的交通；在第三段中討論台灣的海上交通，包括各重要港口及航海線；在第四段中討論台灣的空中交通，包括各機場及航空線；最後在結尾段落中指出台灣的交通確實很發達，而且在政府積極的建設下，等到新的道路系統完成後，必定會更加發達。如此一來，你這篇作文就很有統一性了。

但是，假如你在討論台灣交通的過程中，突然離開主題，高談台灣的教育、工業或農業，那就會破壞這篇作文的統一性了。

第二節　作文的連貫性

在基礎入門篇的第四章第一節中，我們已經討論過句子的連貫性，在第五章第四節中，討論過段落的連貫性，現在要討論整篇作文的連貫性。為了要達到段落的連貫性，必須將一段當中的各個細節按照時間、空間或邏輯的順序排列，並利用承轉詞、代名詞或別的片語把各個句子啣接起來，使之條理分明。整篇作文的連貫性也是如此，只是範圍擴大了，也就是說，一篇作文的各段，也必須按照上面三種順序排列，各段的首尾也要用具有承轉作用的字或片語來啣接，使各段之間能脈絡一貫，通順流暢。比方說，你要是以「台灣的風景名勝」為題寫一篇作文，那你不妨按照空間的順序來敘述台灣各地的風景名勝。你可以在第一段中概括地指出台灣的風景十分美麗；然後按照由北而南的順序，在第二段中敘述台灣北部的風景名勝，包括國父紀念館、中正紀念堂、故宮博物院、陽明山、野柳、石門水庫、烏來等；在第三段中敘述台灣中部的風景名勝，包括溪頭、日月潭、谷關、梨山等；在第四段中敘述台灣南部的風景名勝，包括赤崁樓、澄清湖、佛光山、墾丁公園、鵝鑾鼻等；在第五段中敘述台灣東部的風景名勝，包括鯉魚潭、天祥、太魯閣等；最後在結尾段落中指出台灣的確是個風景如畫、令人流連忘返的寶島。像這樣，你這篇作文就很有連貫性了。不過，假如你在敘述台灣的風景名勝的過程中，忽而北、忽而南、忽而東、忽而西，那你的作文就會顯得雜亂無章、支離破碎，缺少連貫性了。

一般說來，在各段的首尾使用具有承轉作用的字或片語來啣接，

可使一篇作文更為通順流暢。如果你的作文與時間的順序有關，可以在各段的開頭用 first, soon afterward, a little later, then finally 之類的字或片語來啣接。如果是在議論中提出若干論點，則可在各段中用 in the first place, in like manner, moreover 等來啣接。如果是相反的說法，則可在各段中用 on the other hand, however 等來連接。不過，在一篇比較短的作文中，這類具有承轉作用的字或片語不能用得太多。

現在以下面這篇作文為例，說明怎樣在各段之間使用具有承轉作用的字或片語，以達到通順流暢、更為連貫的效果：

The sky above the quaint little Swiss winter resort was covered with heavy, sad-looking clouds. The air was crisp and cold, and, although conditions were perfect, few skiers were out on the snow-covered hills. But **my father** had decided that this should be **the day** when he would **go skiing** with his ten year old **son**.

We didn't have to wait long in front of the suntanned wooden hut which housed the **ski lift's bottom station**. Presently, we were standing side by side on the track, waiting for the hook, shaped like a reversed clothes hanger, to be put under our seats by an attendant. We slid a few yards and —whoop, there went the hook snapping in the air. This meant we had to start over again. Once more we stood next

to each other, waiting. The awkward maneuver worked even worse the second time and we stumbled to the ground. Again we tried—and went sprawling. Finally we decided to **travel separately**.

Alone, it went beautifully, and, with no effort at all, **I was carried** up the steep, long mountain. The white-capped fir trees looked down on me with a friendly smile, as if to say, "So you finally made it!" I glanced behind me to see whether my father was following me, but there was no sign of him. "Well," I thought, "I'll meet **him at the top**."

Five minutes, ten minutes later—no **father** was being pulled up the **last steep stretch of the track**. Apparently, he couldn't even ride the ski lift alone. After at least another twenty people had made it to the top, I decided not to wait any longer and descend by myself. But which way? It was the first time I was on this mountain and the way down was not marked. The only solution I could think of was to **take the same route I had used to go up**.

There was no trail **along the track of the ski lift** and the snow was soft, deep, and dangerous. The slope was getting so steep that I had to take off my

skis and try to stagger downhill. With every aching step, I sank to my knees. As if my misery wasn't complete, it began to snow with thick, clinging flakes. Soon my legs were numb and I could barely move. I must have tortured myself for half an hour when I heard a yell. It was one of the attendants from the bottom station. He guided me out of the drifts and, after a short rest, took me down the wide, easy trail **back to the hut**.

Once I was **deposited before a roaring fire**, my boots were off in no time and I began to thaw out with a cup of hot tea. My father, rather guiltily, put a heavy hand on my shoulder and said, "Next time, son, you won't have to fight both me and the slope."

上面這篇作文一共有六段，每段都有一些黑體字，這些黑體字便表示前後各段之間的關係：第二段開頭一句中的We及ski lift's bottom station便和第一段末尾一句中的 my father, go skiing 及 son 互相呼應。第三段開頭一句中的 Alone...,I was carried 便和第二段末尾的 travel separately 密切關聯；第四段開頭一句中的 father... last steep stretch of the track 也和第三段末尾的 him at the top有密切關係；第五段開頭一句中的along the track of the ski lift便和第四段末尾的take the same route I had used to go up 連成一氣；第六段開頭一句中的

deposited before a roaring fire表示作者像第五段末尾所說的,已經 back to the hut 了。

第三節　適當的強調

一篇好的作文的題材，須用心安排，以求獲得適當的強調。此種強調可以用篇幅的分配（Proportion）、重覆（Repetition）和位置（Position）來表示。

1.　用篇幅的分配來表示強調：將整篇作文的篇幅就各個不同的部分作適當的分配，便可以達到強調的目的。不十分重要但卻用得著的題材，應該佔比較小的篇幅；重要的題材自然應該佔比較大的篇幅。

2.　用重覆來表示強調：實際上，「重覆」本身已經具有強調的作用。在不同的地方就某一重要論點一再作合理的重覆，便可以收到強調的效果。但是，要避免不合理或不必要的重覆，否則就會變得廢字連篇、枯燥無味。

3.　用位置來表示強調：最能表示強調的位置的是在一篇作文的末尾，其次是在一篇作文的開頭。一篇好的作文，開頭的語氣要強，結尾的語氣要更強。比方說，在一篇作文中討論颱風或洪水之類的天然災害時，最好按照「由輕而重」的順序來討論：首先討論財產的損害，其次討論疾病的發生，最後討論生命的喪失。

練 習 二

　　下面三段係摘錄自一篇作文，首先在使各段相互啣接的字或片語下面畫底線，然後在各段中使各句互相啣接的字或片語下面畫底線：

　　A new-born baby girl is unaware of the world about her. So far as she is concerned, existence consists of sleeping, drinking milk from a bottle, and being changed.The helpless tot doesn't hear very well, sees rather poorly, and cannot speak at all. Certainly, the phenomenon of sound has not yet interested her.

　　After a few weeks, her sensitivity toward sound awakens. Apparently, she begins to be conscious of her parents' voices. They talk to her and she looks back as if she understands. Later, she becomes interested in toys that make noise. At first, a new rattle from grandma frightens her. But she gets used to it and shakes it at all hours. Yes, she seems to say, sound is fun.

　　At three months, she becomes keenly aware of special sounds about her. A puppy's bark, the

television set in another room, the thunder on a stormy night, the chatter of birds on a bright, sunny morning—all these have a visible effect upon baby. One day she discovers that she can make her own sounds. She laughs when she is tickled, cries when she is hungry, and gurgles to herself in the secret language of infants. Now sound has become part of her inner and outer life.

第四章　範文

Ⅰ．描寫文（Descriptive Essays）

1. Our Next-Door Neighbors

" Good fences make good neighbors " [1] runs the proverb; how true this is may be realized from our experience of those people next door.

The characteristic of our neighbors that first leaps to mind[2] is their capacity for borrowing. No sooner has Mrs. Chang borrowed a bottle of milk——" the milkman forgot us this morning, Mrs. Huang " ——than [3] she is seen again pushing her way [4] through our hedges to borrow a box of cube sugar——" to save me from [5] going out today." This tendency is also evident in Miss Chang, who [6] is constantly borrowing my bicycle, and even in Baby Precious, who 'borrows,' but never returns, the toys I no longer [7] play with but prefer to keep for old times' sake.

Added to this is their capacity for creating noise. It does not matter what day it is or what time of day,[8] they just love to make noise. Indeed it almost seems to be a matter of planning so that [9] they may obtain the moments most fitting to disturb their neighbors. Thus early in the morning before we are up, and late at night just as we are trying to fall asleep, are selected times for their noisy living room concerts. Sunday morning is a particularly favorite time for turning up [10] their stereo system,[11] though this sound is sometimes accompanied by simultaneous blasts on Billy Chang's saxophone.

一、近鄰

俗語說：「好籬笆造成的好鄰居」；這句話究竟真實到什麼程度，可以由我們同隔壁鄰居交往的經驗而充分了解。

談到鄰居的特點，最先湧現在我心頭的是他們跟人借東西的本領。張太太 剛剛來借一瓶牛奶（她說「送牛奶的人今天早晨忘記給我們送了，黃太太。」）馬上又從我們的樹籬中間擠過來，向我們借一盒方糖——「免得我今天還要跑出去。」張小姐也很明顯地表現出這種癖性，她經常借我的自行車，甚至小寶貝也是一樣，他常來「借」我的玩具，但總是有借無還，雖然那些玩具我已經不再玩了，但是願意保存起來作個紀念。

除了借東西之外，他們製造噪音的本領也很大。不論是那一天，也不論是一天當中的什麼時候，他們總是喜歡製造噪音。實在說，他們幾乎是經過一番設計，把噪音安排在最能擾亂鄰居的時候。因此，他們選擇大清早我們還未起床的時候，和深夜我們正要入睡的時候，高聲舉行他們的起居室音樂會。他們特別喜歡在禮拜天上午把音響的聲音開得很大，不過有時張比利還在同時吹薩克斯風，當作伴奏。

Another aspect of the Chang's is their attempt to keep up with [12] the Huangs. This is particularly exasperating when we know that we are really superior to [13] our neighbors. Only the other day we had our gate painted a beautiful cinnamon brown,[14] which drew many compliments from passers-by. Next morning, there was Mr. Chang painting his gate in exactly the same color. This was annoying enough but it was the last straw [15] when he said that he had had the idea ages ago but that we had " beat him to the punch. " [16] It was the same with our television set. Our twenty-one inch screen was followed immediately by theirs, our new washing machine by theirs, and our Yue Loong[17] by an identical one for the Changs.

A further habit of theirs, which we find so displeasing, is their readiness to give opinions, particularly when they are in reference to [18] some shortcoming of ours. Mrs. Chang is forever telling Mother how to cook roast duck and what the best way to make spiced sausages is. She never wearies of repeating her receipes. Father has been told dozens of times that his garden is backward and that the only way to get plump tomatoes is to use 'Tai Nung Fertilizer.' Their advice even extends to me. I am tired of [19] the number of times I have been told by Billy Chang that I do not know how to dribble a basketball, especially when I know that he failed to make the high school basketball team [20] during tryouts [21] last year.

Finally there are the neighbor's pets. We are as fond as anyone of [22] animals but we believe that they should be kept in their place. Not so the Changs : they believe their pets should have free access not only to [23] their own, but to our backyard garden in particular. Their cat, Charlie, has ruined Father's seedlings, and their dog, Whitey, has dug innumerable holes for his bones. On the whole, therefore, we feel we suffer much from

　　張家的另一個特性，是總想事事不要落在黃家之後。有時候，我們知道自己確實比鄰居們強，他們那種作風特別使人惱火。就在前幾天，我們把大門漆成很漂亮的紅褐色，引起了過路人的許多稱讚。第二天早晨，張先生把他的大門也漆成完全一樣的顏色。這件事情已經夠使人生氣了，但是他還說他老早就打算把大門漆成這個顏色，想不到被我們「搶先」了，這種說法真把人氣壞了，使我們無法再容忍下去。關於電視機的情形也是一樣。我們買了一架二十一吋的電視機，他們馬上照樣買了一架，我們買了一台新洗衣機，他們也買了一台，我們買了一輛裕隆轎車，張家也馬上買了一輛完全相同的轎車。

　　他們還有一種習慣，使我們極感不快，就是好發表意見，特別是和我們的某項缺點有關的事情。張太太不斷地告訴母親怎樣做烤鴨，和做香腸的最佳方法。她總在重覆講述她的烹飪法，永不厭倦。張先生時常告訴父親說他的菜園太落伍了，要想使番茄長得肥大，唯有使用「台農肥料」。他們對各種事情都有建議，連我也逃脫不了。張比利不斷地告訴我說我不會運球，其次數之多，令我感到厭煩，尤其是當我知道他在去年的選拔賽中未能入選籃球校隊的時候。

　　最後要說的，就是張家所養的寵物了。我們喜歡動物，不遜於任何人，但是我們認為應該把動物放在適當的處所。張家的人卻不這樣想，他們認為他們的寵物不僅可以自由進入他們後院的菜園，更可以自由進入我們後院的菜園。他們的貓查理把父親種植的幼苗都毀壞了，他們的狗小白在後院挖了無數的洞，埋藏牠的骨頭。因此，大體說來，我們覺得隔壁一家使我們受了許多罪。

the people next door.

Yet it is a sobering thought that, if they moved, I suppose we would miss them. I know that when they went traveling during summer vacation last year, I felt lonely for the whole time.

　　可是，平心靜氣地想一想，如果他們搬走了，我們會想念他們。我記得，在去年暑假他們全家外出旅行的期間，我一直覺得很寂寞。

注解：

(1) **Good fences make good neighbors:** fences or walls between our properties are not just physical barriers; they are a reminder to both of us that a good neighbor should never be obtrusive. 好籬笆造成好鄰居。這句話的意思是說：兩家之間的籬笆或牆不僅是實體的障礙物，也具有一種心理上的功用，提醒我們要想做一個好鄰居，就永遠不要妨礙住在隔壁的人們。

(2) **leap to mind:** come suddenly to mind; occur suddenly to one. 湧現在心頭；忽然想起。

A great idea has just *leapt to mind*——we can give her a surprise party!

我剛剛想到一個好主意——我們可以為她舉行一次使她驚喜的慶祝會！

(3) **no sooner... than:** as soon as... 一…馬上就。

We had *no sooner* sat down *than* she burst into tears.

(=As soon as we sat down, she burst into tears.)

我們剛坐下，她就哭了起來。

No sooner had he seen me *than* he ran off.

他一看到我就跑開了。

(4) **push one's way:** advance by effort, esp. by pushing someone or something aside. 很費力地前進(如藉著把旁人或旁的東西推

開)。

The boy *pushed his way* through the crowd to his father, who was standing on the platform.

那男孩擠過人群，朝著站在台上的父親走去。

(5) **save... from: a**. make unnecessary for; enable one to avoid.

使無須；使避免。

A good dictionary will *save* you *from* making mistakes about the correct meaning of words.

一部好的字典能使你查到正確的字義而不會犯錯。

b. make or keep safe from (injury, loss, etc.)

使免於(傷害，損失等)。

He *saved* the boy *from* drowning. 他使那男孩免遭溺死。

(6) **who:**注意關係代名詞(relative pronoun)引導出一個形容詞子句的用法，這種句法是中文裡面所沒有的。例如：

I met Tom, *who* told me the news.

我遇到湯姆，他告訴我這消息。

We have decided to hire Mrs. Jackson, *who* knows how to cook.

我們決定雇用賈克遜太太，她會做飯。

在這兩個句子裡，由關係代名詞所引導出來的形容詞子句和它所修飾的名詞之間有一個逗點，這種形容詞子句是非限制性的(nonrestrictive),可有可無。如果中間不用逗點，那個形容詞子句就是限制性的(restrictive),不可缺少。試比較下列兩句：

I will employ a man *who* can speak English.

我要雇用一個能說英語的人。

I will employ John, *who* can speak English.

我要雇用約翰，他會說英語。

(7) **no longer:** not any more; not at the present. 不再。

She was *no longer* upset. 她不再心煩了。

We will *no longer* live in this house.

我們再也不會住在這房子裡了。

(8) **(the) time of day:** the hour of the day as shown by the clock.

時辰。

注意：day 之前不用the。

(9) **so that:** with the purpose that; in order that. 為了；以便。

Finish this *so that* you can start another.

把這個做完，以便開始另一個。

I'll give you all the facts *so that* you can judge for yourself.

我將把所有的事實提供給你，讓你自己去判斷。

(10) **turn up:** increase the loudness, intensity, flow, speed, etc. of, as by turning a control; make(a radio, television, etc.)louder.

使…的音量、強度、流量、速度等增加(如藉著轉動控制器)；把(電視、收音機等)的聲音開得更大。

You may *turn up* the television in the early evening, but should turn it down after ten o'clock. 在夜晚七、八點的時候你可以把電視開大聲一點，但在十點以後應該開得小一點。

(11) **stereo system**(stereo: short form of stereophonic):

（一套二聲道的）音響。

(12) **keep up with: a.** try not to be outdone socially or financially by one's neighbor or by others regarded as one's social equal. 在社交和經濟條件的表現方面不使鄰人或具有同等社交地位者勝過自己，與鄰居比闊或比時髦。

The poor fellow nearly went broke because his wife was always trying to *keep up with* their new neighbors.

那個可憐的傢伙幾乎破產了，因為他老婆總跟新來的鄰居比闊、比時髦。

b. go or move as fast as; maintain a similar position to.

與…以同樣速度前進；不落…之後；與…保持同樣地位。

Helen works so fast that no one in the office can *keep up with* her.

海倫工作的速度非常快，辦公室裡沒有人能趕得上她。

(13) **superior to:** superior 和 inferior 當作「優於」或「不如」解時，後面接用 to。

His style is *superior to* that of any other writer of his time.

他的風格優於同時代其他作家的風格。

(14) **cinnamon brown:** reddish brown (cinnamon:肉桂；肉桂色)。

紅褐色。

(15) **the last straw:** the last of a succession of irritations that strains one's patience to the limit. 一連串氣人的事情當中的最後一件，使人無法再心忍受下去。

(16) **beat one to the punch:** do something before another person has had a chance to do it; outdo someone else by taking advantage of an opportunity before he can. 搶先；捷足先登。

(17) **Yue Loong:** 裕隆汽車。

(18) **in (or with) reference to:** regarding; concerning. 關於。

I have nothing to say *in reference to* your question.

關於你的問題，我沒有話說。

I have made all possible inquiries *in reference to* this matter.

關於這件事，我已經作過一切可能的調查。

(19) **be tired of :** have had enough of; be irritated or annoyed by; become weary of. 厭惡；厭煩；厭倦。

Richard *is tired of* eating fried rice for lunch every day.

理查每天中午吃炒飯，已經吃厭了。

I'*m tired of* hearing the same old excuses.

我聽夠了這些同樣的老藉口。

(20) **make the team:** be selected as a team member after passing a skills test. (通過技能測驗之後)成為隊員。

After months of practice, he finally *made the* swimming *team*.

經過幾個月的練習之後，他終於成為游泳隊的隊員。

(21) **tryout:** an opportunity to prove, or a test to determine, one's ability for a place on an athletic team, a role in a play, etc. 選拔。

(22) **be fond of :** have a liking for ; take pleasure in. 喜歡；愛好。

Bob *is fond of* music. 鮑伯愛好音樂。

He *is* very *fond of* his cousin. 他很喜歡他的表妹

(23) **have access to:** have the right, permission, or means to. 有權利或方法進入(某處)或使用(某物)；被許可進入(某處)或使用(某物)。

The secretary *has* exclusive *access to* her boss's files. 秘書有使用老闆檔案的特權。

怎樣寫好 英文 作文

評釋:

　　用一句諺語作為文章的開頭，不失為一個好辦法。

　　這篇作文是有計劃的。最能代表這家鄰居的特性的有下列幾點：好借東西、製造噪音、模仿別人、表示意見、放任寵物等。本文分別在每一段就一個項目加以描述。

　　每段的開頭都有一個主題句。

　　注意本文蘊含的幽默意味。在這種文章裡，切忌使用尖刻的譏諷語句。

練 習 三

A.　根據本課內容，用完整的句子回答下列各問題：

1.　What are some characteristics of the writer's neighbors?

2.　What kinds of things do they borrow?

3.　How do they create a lot of noise?

4.　How do the Changs keep up with the Huangs?

5.　What kinds of opinions do the Changs give to the Huangs?

6.　Why doesn't the writer like the Changs's pets?

7.　Why does the writer suppose he would miss the Changs if they moved?

B. 將下列各句譯成英文，儘量使用本課學過的成語：

1. 關於那件事情我所知道的一切,我都已經告訴你了。

2. 我們去看張先生,他熱誠地歡迎我們。

3. 他剛一到就病了。

4. 我救了他,免於一死。

5. 他在班上功課趕不上。

6. 這本書的文體優於那本書。

7. 我起得很早,為的是可以趕上第一班火車。

8. 她喜歡讀書。

9. 這些貨物比樣品低劣。

10. 我每天早晨吃煮雞蛋都吃厭了。

11. 他不再是個青年了。

C. 任選一題，作短文一篇：

1. People I Meet on the Bus

2. My Best Friend

2. Moving House

After weeks of domestic unrest, of trial and discomfort, the day for moving has at last [1] arrived.

Breakfast this morning has been hastily arranged — a bowl of soybean milk, a piece of bread and jam eaten from a packing carton with a newspaper tablecloth. In any case,[2] we are much too excited to [3] eat, for the moving van has just pulled up [4] outside.

Mother is very busy stuffing packing paper into the bowls and cups, while Father is banging nails into a wooden case full of [5] books and magazines. Both are issuing inaudible [6] orders to my brother and me as we noisily make sure [7] that our favorite keepsakes are not left behind.[8]

A loud banging at the door announces the arrival of the moving men. They enter, full of hearty, good humor; and they display an obvious willingness to lighten our burden by taking full responsibility for the move. Despite this, Father and Mother cannot help fussing [9] and adding pleas for caution as armfuls of their treasured possessions disappear inside the van. Wedding presents of some twenty years' standing particularly come into this category.

We lend a hand, [10] though it is doubtful whether we are a help or a hindrance. I make sure that my 'ten-speed'[11] is safely packed while my younger brother sees that [12] his baseball equipment is not forgotten. The kindly conversation of the moving men keeps us all in good spirits and makes the task of loading the van seem easier.

There is a constant patter of feet on the now-bare floors with such accompanying cries of " A bit to the left, Bill ! " or " Easy as she goes,[13] John! " as the furniture in the bedroom is tackled. A noise like thunder

二、搬家

　　家中經過好幾星期的紛亂不安、磨難和不舒適,搬家的日子終於來臨了。

　　早餐是匆匆忙忙準備起來的—— 每人一碗豆漿,麵包果醬,在包裝紙箱上面鋪一張報紙,當作餐桌。無論如何,我們都太興奮了,沒有心情吃飯,因為搬家車已經停在外面了。

　　母親在忙著把包裝紙塞在碗和杯子裡面,父親則在往一個裝滿了書籍雜誌的木箱上面釘釘子。他們兩人都在向弟弟和我發出一些命令,當時我們正在吵吵鬧鬧地想要確實查明,使我們那些心愛的紀念品不要忘記帶走,因此根本沒有聽清楚他們的吩咐。

　　砰砰敲門的聲音,宣告搬家工人的到達。他們走進來,態度爽朗,心情愉快,並且顯示出一種明顯的意願,想要負起搬家工作的全部責任,藉以減輕我們的負擔。儘管如此,當工人把一包一包的貴重物品放進車裡面的時候,父親和母親還是免不了很緊張,並且關照工人多加小心。他們已經保存了二十年左右的結婚禮物,尤其屬於此類貴重物品。

　　我們也都幫忙了,不過我們究竟是真的幫忙了,還是越幫越忙,就很難說了。我要照看一下,使我那輛「十段變速自行車」確實很穩妥地裝在車上了,我弟弟則在注意使他的棒球用具不被遺忘。搬家工人的親切談話使我們大家的心情都很高興,並且使裝車的工作似乎更為容易。

　　在現在已經光禿的地板上,不斷發出急速的腳步聲,在搬運臥室家具的時候,總有人大聲關照:「稍微偏左一點兒,比爾!」或「多加小心,慢慢的,約翰!」一個如雷的響聲告訴我們在搬運主臥

tells us that some mishap has occurred in the handling of the bed in the master bedroom. It is now that we notice clouds of dust beginning to fill the air, and our noses respond with frequent sneezes.

By this time a crowd of interested bystanders has gathered around the van, most of them my friends from the neighborhood; to them such a sight is a form of free entertainment in their rather uneventful lives. Their curiosity sometimes gets the better of [14] them and a gruff voice is occasionally necessary to keep them at a distance.[15]

Father makes a last, careful inspection of the premises, looking into [16] every corner and cupboard. He sees that the windows are fastened, the faucets are turned off,[17] and that the doors to the balcony and back porch are secure. He puts on [18] his coat and takes one final look.

Eventually the house is empty, and before the key is turned in the front door for the last time, I linger in the living room for a nostalgic [19] minute. It is an exciting but sad moment as I reflect on [20] the incidents which have taken place [21] in that house during the past ten years of my young life. I give a shrug, whistle for the dog, and join the rest of my family in the taxi which follows the van to our new house.

室的床的時候發生了事故。現在我們發覺一陣陣的灰塵開始充塞在空氣之中,我們的鼻子時常打噴嚏。

這時候,一群看熱鬧的人已經聚集在搬家車的四周,他們大部分是住在附近一帶的朋友;對他們來說,這個場面可以說是他們的相當平靜無事的生活當中的一種免費娛樂。他們有時完全為好奇心所驅使著,必須有人用粗率的聲音使他們保持相當的距離。

父親對整個家宅很仔細地做了最後一次的視察,把每一個角落和每一個壁櫥都查看了。他要整個檢查一遍,務必使窗戶都關牢了,龍頭都關閉起來了,通到陽臺和後門廊的門都關好了。他穿上外衣,最後又四下看了一看。

整個房屋終於都搬空了,在把前門最後一次地鎖起之前,我在起居室逗留片刻,對這所房屋發抒一些懷戀之情。我回想過去十載的童年生活當中在這所房屋裡所發生的種種事情,心頭感到既興奮又憂愁。我聳聳肩膀,吹口哨把我的狗喊來,上了計程車,和家人會合。那輛計程車跟在搬家車之後,朝著我們的新居駛去。

注解:

(1) **at last:** in the end; after much delay. 最後；終於。

The holidays came *at last*. 假期終於來到。

He was lost in thought for several minutes, but *at last* he spoke.

他沉思了幾分鐘，但最後說話了。

(2) **in any case:** whatever happens or may have happened; under any circumstances. 無論如何。

We have to help him to pay the debt *in any case*.

我們無論如何都要幫他還債。

(3) **too... to:** 太…不。

The tea is *too* hot *to* drink. 茶太燙，不能喝。

The book is *too* difficult for me *to* read.

這本書太難，我看不懂。

The news is *too* good *to* be true.

這消息太好了，實在叫人難以相信。

This was *too* great an honor not *to* excite the envy of his rivals.

這是一個極大的榮譽，不會不引起他的競爭者們的嫉妒。

He is *too* wise not *to* see that.

以他的聰明，不會看不出那種情形。

(4) **pull up :** come to a stop. 停下。

The taxi *pulled up* in front of the hotel.

計程車在旅社前面停下。

He *pulled up* at the front gate. 他把車子開到大門口停下。

(5) **full of :** filled with. 充滿。

Her bedroom is *full of* dolls. 她的臥室裡滿是洋娃娃。

His life is *full of* trouble 。 他的一生充滿憂患。

(6) **inaudible:** incapable of being heard clearly (because of noise, distance, etc.) . 聽不清楚。

(7) **make sure:** be certain; do what is necessary in order to feel sure, to get something, etc. 務必；查明；弄清楚。

Make sure that you finish your assignment on time.

務必要準時做完你的作業。

Please *make sure* that you have not made any spelling errors.

請弄清楚，不要有拼字的錯誤。

(8) **leave behind:** not to take with one at departure; neglect or forget to bring or take. 忘記帶走；遺留。

The baggage has been *left behind*. 行李忘記帶走了。

Take care not to *leave* anything *behind*.

千萬不要遺留任何東西。

(9) **cannot help (-ing):** be unable to refrain from (doing something).

不能不；不禁（後面接用 gerund, 即動詞的-ing 形式）。

I *can't help* thinking he's still alive. 我總覺得他還活著。

Sharon *could not help* laughing. 霞倫不禁大笑起來。

(10) **lend a hand:** a help; give assistance. 幫忙；協助。

Jerry saw a woman having difficulty changing a flat tire and offered to *lend* her *a hand*.

傑瑞看見一位婦人換跑氣的輪胎有困難，於是自動去幫她忙。

I would not have finished my homework today if Allen hadn't *lent* me *a hand*.

要不是愛倫幫我忙，我今天就做不完我的作業了。

(11) **ten-speed:** a kind of racing bicycle with ten speeds.

十段變速自行車（一種跑車）。

(12) **see that:** give attention or care to; make sure that.

務必使；注意使。

See that your homework is finished before you go out to play.

在你出去玩之前，一定要把作業作完。

I will *see that* it is done according to your directions.

我一定會注意使這件事按照你的指示做。

Steve *saw that* the matter was handled promptly.

史迪夫已負責照料將這件事迅速處理。

(13) **Easy as she goes:** Do it carefully, without sudden movements and without forcing too hard or fast. 小心；慢慢來。

"*Easy as she goes,* " said the fisherman as they raised the net out of the water.

他們把網拖出水來的時候，漁夫說道：「小心，慢慢來。」

(14) **get the better of:** overcome; defeat (someone) or deal successfully with (a difficulty). 克服；打敗；勝過。

His shyness *got the better of* him. 他很害羞。

George *got the better of* Robert in a game of Chinese chess.
喬治在象棋比賽中勝了羅伯。

(15) **keep... at a distance:** prevent... from coming too close, esp. from becoming too friendly.

與…保持距離；不與接近。

The old man doesn't like little children and tries to *keep* them *at a distance*. 那老人不喜歡小孩子,所以不想跟他們親近.

Mr. Jones is kind to the workers in his store, but after work he *keeps* them *at a distance*.

鍾斯先生在店裡對工作人員很好,可是下班以後不大和他們親近.

(16) **look into:** inspect; examine; investigate. 調查;察看;視察。

The police are *looking into* the past record of the man.
警察局正在調查那人過去的記錄。

(17) **turn off :** stop the flow of (liquid, gas, electrical current, etc.) by turning a tap, pressing a switch, etc. 關閉。

Please *turn off* the lights before you go to bed.
睡覺前請把燈關掉。

注意：turn off 的相對語是 turn on , 參看範文 17，注 7。

(18) **put on:** clothe with. 穿上；戴上。

He *put on* his hat and coat and went out.

他戴上帽子，穿上外套，然後走了出去

(19) **nostalgic:** of feeling, or causing nostalgia (nostalgia : a fond desire for some experience, thing, person, or time which one had personal knowledge of). 懷舊的，懷念過去的。

I had a *nostalgic* moment when I saw that lake again.

我再度看到那個湖的時候，不禁記起過去的一切。

She was filled with *nostalgia* when she heard that old record.

她聽到那舊唱片時，往事湧上心頭。

(20) **reflect on:** consider carefully; think on. 考慮；思考。

I must *reflect on* what you said.

我得考慮考慮你所說的話。

The President is *reflecting on* the matter before making a decision.

總統未做決定之前正在考慮這件事。

(21) **take place:** happen; occur. 發生；舉行。

When will the football match *take place*? 足球賽何時舉行?

The meeting *took place* in the auditorium. 會議在禮堂舉行。

評釋：

　　本文描述一項經驗，或某時某地所發生的事情和在場的人們的情形。

　　起頭是開門見山式的，用一句簡單明瞭的話做開端，然後按照時間順序描述一件一件的事情。先描述匆忙的早飯，再描述父母在做些什麼，然後搬家的工人來了，作者告訴我們，他們和全家的人都在做些什麼，直到最後，搬運車駛走，全文很自然地結束了。

　　這種題目如果用純記敘的方式寫，讀起來會很乏味。本文實在可以說是一篇半記敘半描寫的文章。

　　末段的 nostalgic minute 一語為本文增加一些情趣，供人回味。

　　本文內容是過去的事情，為敘述生動起見，動詞都用現在式。在文法上，這種用法叫做 historical present（歷史的現在式）。

練　習　四

A.　根據本課內容，用完整的句子回答下列各問題：

1.　What was hastily arranged for breakfast?

2.　Why is everyone too excited to eat breakfast?

3.　What are the writer's mother and father doing?

4.　How do the moving men enter the house? What do they display?

5.　How do the writer and his younger brother lend a hand?

6. Why has a crowd of interested bystanders gathered around the van?

7. How does the writer's father make a last, careful inspection?

8. What does the writer do before the key is turned in the front door for the last time?

9. What does the writer do just before he joins the rest of his family in the taxi?

B. 將下列各句譯成英文，儘量利用本課學過的成語：

1. 請幫我把書架挪一挪。

2. 這個瓶子裡裝滿了墨水。

3. 我要調查這件事。

4. 這個意外事件是在什麼地方發生的？

5. 我不能不認為你是一個惡人。

6. 我要注意把一切事情都安排得很適當。

7. 這張床太短，我睡不下。

8. 他終於做完了他的作業。

9. 無論如何，我總要設法前來。

10. 不要忘記把傘帶走。

11. 我想六點半有一班火車，但是你最好查明白。

12. 你做完飯的時候，把瓦斯關掉。

C. 任選一題，作短文一篇：

1. Scenes at the Train Station

2. Going for a Walk

3. The Pleasures of City Life

Most people like to visit the country, especially on weekends in the summer, but many who live in a large city would dislike the idea of having to[1] live in the country all year round.

To some people the chief pleasure of life in the city lies in [2] its lively tempo [3], which stimulates every cell in one's body. The noise of traffic, of people coming and going in large numbers, is nourishment to the city dweller. He loves companionship and the opportunity for ready friendship, and feels that everyone is so amicable and helpful. Loneliness, the curse [4] of the countryman, seldom affects him.

The ease with which purchases can be made [5] in a big city also adds to [6] the pleasure of its life. If a spare part is wanted, there is never a long delay, for stocks [7] are well supplied; if the latest disco [8] record is desired, it can be purchased at any of hundreds of record stores; if a change in cuisine [9] is longed for[10], there are restaurants specializing in food from almost every province in China to choose from. In fact, variety is the keynote of the city. A whole day may be spent in deciding what kind of shoes or clothes to buy, because there are so many different kinds to choose from.

Then there is the delight of window shopping. Without purchasing a single article, a morning's enjoyment may be had from simply looking at the latest goods displayed in the most tempting manner. At the numerous department stores in the downtown area one can often find quality merchandise at bargain prices.

There is such a variety of entertainment in the city. First-run[11] theaters, amusement centers[12], variely halls[13], bowling alleys[14], and skating

三、城市生活的樂趣。

　　大多數人都喜歡到鄉間作短暫的停留，尤其是在夏季的周末，但是許多住在大城市的人都不願意長年住在鄉間。

　　對某些人來說，城市生活的主要樂趣在於它的活潑輕快的節拍，那種節拍刺激著一個人身體的每個細胞。往來的車輛和大批行人的喧囂，等於是城市居民的營養品(意指為城市繁榮之所繫)。他喜歡交友和馬上可以得到友誼的機會，並且覺得每個人都是非常友善而有幫助的。寂寞是鄉下人生活當中的弊害，卻很少能影響城市居民。

　　在大城市買東西極為方便，這一點也增加了城市生活的樂趣。如果需要一個備用的零件，不必耽擱很久，因為商店裡的存貨很豐富；如果想要最新的狄斯可唱片，在成百家唱片行當中的任何一家都可以買到；如果在飲食方面想換換口味，做每省菜肴的餐館幾乎都有，可供選擇。實際上，變化多端是城市生活的基調。我們可能花費一整天的時間，來決定購買哪一種皮鞋和衣服，可供選擇的種類實在太多了。

　　其次，還有瀏覽商店櫥窗的樂趣。一件東西都不必買，只是觀賞在櫥窗裡面以一種極誘人的方式展示出來的最新貨品，就可以使你很愉快地度過一個上午。在商業區的許多百貨公司裡，你時常可以發現上等品質的廉價貨品。

　　城市裡的娛樂項目非常繁多。有首輪電影院、娛樂中心、歌廳、保齡球場、溜冰場等，居住在城市的人絕對不愁晚上沒有消遣

rinks[15] mean that the city dweller is never at a loss[16] to pass an evening. It does not matter if he is too busy to see a good movie one day; it will be shown at a second-run[17] theater in the near future. If he does not make a new acquaintance one night, there is always the chance that he will do so the next.

The city is so convenient. If Mother wants a plumber, or Father an electrician, a call on the telephone will bring one in an instant. In the country, one may have to wait days for a repairman, or else have to attempt the repair himself at the cost of [18] much of his time and energy. If Mary wants the cosmetics she saw advertised on television one evening, it is a certainty that she will be able to buy them the next day. If little Johnny needs a mechanic for his bicycle, he need only go a short distance before finding a repair shop. If we have no car, convenient busses, trains, and readily available[19] taxis are at our disposal.[20]

Perhaps the greatest pleasure of living in a big city is the happy feeling of being in the know[21]. With all kinds of conveniences and comforts available, the city dweller is living in the mainstream of modern life.

的地方。如果他某一天太忙了，不能去看一部好片子，那也沒有關係，不久那部電影還會在二輪電影院放映。如果他某一天沒能結交一個新朋友，第二天他總會有機會結交。

　　住在城市非常方便。如果母親要找一個鉛管工人，父親要找一個電機匠，打一個電話，他馬上就會來。在鄉下，如果想找一個修理工人，往往要等上好幾天他才能來，否則就得自己動手修理，花費很多時間和體力。如果瑪麗想買某天晚上她在電視廣告上看到的那種化妝品，她第二天必定能夠買到。如果小強尼需要一名機匠修理自行車，他只須走很短的一段路，就能找到一家修理店。如果我們自己沒有汽車，很方便的公共汽車、火車、和很容易叫到的計程車都隨時可供我們使用。

　　居住大城市的最大樂趣，也許是見聞廣博消息靈通的愉快感覺。享有所有各種的便利和舒適，城市居民可以說是置身在現代生活的主流之中。

注解：

(1) **have to:** must; be obliged or forced to. 必須；不得不

Do you *have to* go now? 你一定要現在走嗎?

He's so rich that he doesn't *have to* work.

他非常富有，不必工作。

(2) **lie (in):** exist (in); be found (in). 在於

His greatness *lies* in his character. 他的偉大在於他的品格。

The success of the negotiations *lies* in their willingness to compromise.

談判的成功在於他們的妥協的意願。

(3) **tempo:** the rate of movement or activity. 動作或活動的速度。

(4) **curse:** a cause of unhappiness, misfortune, evil, etc.

禍害；禍根。

Malaria is the *curse* of the tropics. 瘧疾是熱帶地區的禍害。

Foxes can be a *curse* to farmers. 狐狸能成為農人的禍害。

(5) **make a purchase:** buy something. 購買；採購。

I have *some purchases* to *make*. 我要去些東西。

She *made a* good *purchase* in the dress shop.

他在服裝店裡買了一件衣服，質料很好而價錢不貴。

(6) **add to:** increase; produce or serve as an addition to. 增加。

The soft music *added to* the atmosphere of the restaurant.

柔和的音樂增加了餐廳的氣氛。

The accessories *added to* the cost of the car.

附件增加了汽車的費用。

(7) **stock:** a supply of goods kept on hand by a merchant, distributor, etc. for sale to customers. 現貨；存貨。

(8) **disco:** a type of soul music characterized by strong, regular danceable rhythms and simplified lyrics which are repeated over and over again. 狄斯可。

(9) **cuisine:** style of cooking. 烹調；烹飪法。

(10) **long for:** have an earnest or strong desire for; wish for very much. 渴望。

Everyone is *longing for* peace. 人人渴望和平。

The school children are *longing for* summer vacation.

小學生渴望放暑假。

(11) **first-run:** relating to or specializing in the first showings of new motion pictures. 首輪(電影院)。

(12) **amusement center:** 娛樂中心。

(13) **variety hall:** (variety: entertainment of mixed character, consisting of a number of individual performances of acts, as of singing, dancing, acrobatics, playlets, etc.): 綜藝表演廳；歌廳；雜耍場。

(14) **bowling alley:** 保齡球場。

(15) **skating rink:** 溜冰場。

(16) **at a loss:** be perplexed or uncertain (what to do or say).

困惑；不知道 (怎麼辦，說什麼好)。

He was *at a loss* for a suitable reply.

他不知道怎麼作適當的回答。

(17) **second-run:** relating to or specializing in the showing of motion pictures which have been released before (usually in first-run theaters). 二輪(電影院)。

(18) **at the cost of:** at the loss or expense of.

以…為代價；犧牲；損失。

He saved his son from drowning, but only *at the cost of* his own life.

他使他的兒子免遭溺死，卻犧牲了自己的生命。

(19) **readily available:** easily gotten, used, etc.

現成的；隨時可用的。

A wide variety of reference books are *readily available* in the library.

圖書館備有各式各樣的參考書供人使用。

(20) **at one's disposal:** ready for one's use or service at any time.

可供隨時使用；隨時可以提供服務。

He has plenty of money *at his disposal*.

他有很多錢可以使用。

My library is *at your disposal*. 你可以使用我的藏書。

I'm *at your disposal* the whole morning.

我整個早上可以聽你差遣。

(21) **in the know:** well-informed; having more information (about something) than others. 知道內情的。

To those *in the know*, it was obvious which one was better.

對知道內情的人來說，哪一個比較好是顯而易見的。

怎樣寫好 英文 作文

評釋：

注意題目裡面有一個極關重要的字，就是 pleasure。這個題目要我們說的不只是城市生活，而是城市生活的樂趣。

第一段是引言。注意第二、三、四段開頭的寫法。第二段的開頭是 the chief pleasure of life in the city...; 第三段的開頭是 The ease with which purchases can be made in big cities also adds to the pleasure of its life; 第四段的開頭是 Then there is the delight of window shopping.

其他各段也都以類似的方式起頭。

作者對每個項目都提出了充分的證明，使讀者信服。

練 習 五

A. 根據本課內容，用完整的句子回答下列各問題：

1. In what does the chief pleasure of city life lie?

2. What is nourishment to the city dweller?

3. How does the ease with which purchases can be made add to the pleasures living in the city?

4. What is the delight of window shopping?

5. What can one do for entertainment in the big city?

6. In what ways is living in the city very convenient?

7. What is the greatest pleasure of living in a big city?

B. 將下列各句譯成英文，儘量利用本課學過的成語：

1. 這筆錢可由我們支配。

2. 我不知說什麼好。

3. 他犧牲榮譽而獲得了財富。

4. 我渴望有機會和你見面。

5. 在你需要他的時候，他總是隨時會來幫忙。

6. 我必須早些離去。

7. 他的病增加了家人的苦惱。

8. 她的嫵媚(attractiveness)在於她的眼睛。

C. 任選一題，作短文一篇：

1. The Attraction of a Large Park

2. The Function of Museums

4. The Fascination of a Large Department Store

To go inside the China Department Store is to step into a wonderland.

There is such a wide variety of goods that we cannot help but[1] be fascinated by them. For instance, there is the handicraft department with its glazed ceramic vases and porcelain tea sets which twinkle in the display lights.[2] Here all shapes of the craftsman's skill are on display, from green jade figurines to imitation Ch'ing snuff bottles [3]. It is easy to lose all track of [4] time just by investigating the shapes alone, admiring their detail and the patience with which they were made. Attracted by their brilliant colors, we are tempted to feel each piece individually, even at the risk of being warned by the alert salesgirl of their fragileness. In contrast with this department is that of housewares, with its stylish dinnerware——white dishes with modest pale-blue edging, and intricately carved ivory chopsticks—neatly arranged on embroidered silk tablecloths.

Part of the fascination of the department store lies [5] in the multitude of items for sale under one roof. On one floor we find sporting goods side by side with camera equipment, pendant lamps of every shape and color competing with attractive pens and stationery, watches and pocket calculators sitting back to back with radios and tape recorders, and microwave ovens striving with television sets for preeminence. There is so much order in disorder.

The atmosphere, too, is one not experienced elsewhere and adds to [6] the attractiveness of the store. Everyone is so busy coming and going: untiring escalators [7] silently move their way up and down; elevators load and unload; sales personnel dart here and there, and customer bumps

四、大百貨公司的魔力

走進中華百貨公司，等於步入一個奇境。

貨品的種類極為繁多，使我們不能不為之著迷。例如，在手工藝品部裡，有上釉的陶瓷花瓶和瓷製茶具，在聚光燈下面閃爍發光。在這裡，表現工匠技巧的所有各種形狀，從碧玉的小雕像以至清朝鼻煙壺的仿製品，都陳列出來了，只是察看那些物品的形狀，欣賞他們的細節和匠人製作時所下的工夫，就很容易完全忘記時間的消逝。我們被那些燦爛的顏色吸引著，不禁去把每件東西都摸一摸，甚至甘冒被留心的女店員警告的危險，她們會告訴我們說那些東西很容易破碎。和這個形成一個對照的，是家庭用具部，那裡有很考究的餐具，帶有淡藍色素邊的盤子，雕刻細緻的象牙筷子，很整齊地排列在一個繡花的網桌布面上。

這家百貨公司的魔力，一部分在於出售物品的繁多。在某一層樓上，我們發現運動用品同照像器材並排陳列，各種形狀和顏色的吊燈同吸引的鋼筆和文具互爭短長，錶和袖珍計算機擺在收音機和錄音機的旁邊，微波爐同電視機彼此爭勝。在紊亂之中呈現著良好的秩序。

這裡的氣氛也是在別處感受不到的，更為增長了這家百貨公司的吸引力。大家忙著來來去去：永不倦怠的自動梯默默地上上下下，電梯的乘客進進出出，店員以快速的步伐各處走動，顧客在寬廣的樓梯上面摩肩接踵。

customer on the wide stairs.

Yet by contrast there is no need for the prospective buyer to hurry. Indeed, this is one of the major attractions of the store——we need not buy anything at all. Occasionally, someone will ask us if we are being assisted or if she can help us, but on the whole [8] we can spend an entire day there just passing the time away. We can move from department to department at our own sweet will.[9] Not only can we shop there, but in the amusement center we can even sharpen our mental dexterity by playing one of the latest electronic games. If we wish to take a brief rest from the eye-filling[10] sights, we may sip Colombian coffee in a cozy coffee shop, enjoy fragrant tea and tasty snacks at a Cantonese restaurant, or even have a full-course [11] meal in one of the several restaurants on the upper floors. The prices are reasonable, and the cuisine, superb. We can even enjoy a first-run[12] movie in one of the plush [13] theaters located in this miniature city.

Some may feel that a baseball game has all the merits of good entertainment, others a variety show or a concert; but to many of us no place is more fascinating than a large department store.

　　可是，在比照之下，可能的購物者欲無須匆忙。實在說，這是這家百貨公司的主要吸引力之一——我們可以不必購買任何東西。有時候，會有店員詢問是否已有其他店員為我們服務，要不要她幫忙，但是大體說來，我們可以在百貨公司裡待一整天，僅僅為了消磨時間。我們可以隨心所欲地從一個部門走到另一個部門。我們不僅可以在那裡買東西，吃飯，還可以在娛樂中心玩最新的電子遊戲，藉以增長心智的靈敏。如果那些琳琅滿目的景象使你覺得累了，想休息一下，你可以到一家舒適的咖啡館裡喝哥倫比亞咖啡，或到一家廣東餐館喝香茶，吃美味的點心，甚或到上層的數家餐廳之中的一家，吃一頓全餐。價錢都很公道，烹調技術極佳。這座小型城市裡面還有幾家豪華的戲院，我們可以在那裡看一場首輪電影。

　　有些人也許認為棒球比賽具有良好娛樂一切優點。有些人也許認為綜藝表演和音樂會是最好的消遣，但是對我們當中的許多人來說，大百貨公司實在是一個最吸引人的場所。

注解：

(1) **cannot help but:** cannot avoid (-ing). 不得不。

When the streets are under repair, you *cannot help but* get your shoes muddy. 街道在整修時，你的鞋上一定會黏滿泥。

I *cannot help but* go out in the bad weather.

我不得不冒著風雨外出。

(2) **display light:** 聚光燈。

(3) **imitation Ch'ing snuff bottle:** 仿製的清朝鼻煙壺。

(4) **lose track of :** fail to keep informed about; forget about; lose touch with.

不能繼續熟悉…的情形；同…失去聯繫。

She bought so many Christmas presents that she completely *lost track of* how much money she spent.

她買了很多聖誕禮物，根本記不清到底花了多少錢。

Billy *lost track of* his classmates after graduating from college.

比利大學畢業後跟班上同學失去聯繫。

lose track of 的相對語是 keep track of。

(5) **lie in:** 參看範文 3，注 2。

(6) **add to:** 參看範文 3，注 6。

(7) **escalator:** a continuously moving stairway for carrying people up or down. 自動梯。

(8) **on the whole:** in general ; taking everything into consideration.

整個看起來;大體上。

On the whole it seemed best to cut the visit short.

大體來說,最好把這次遊覽縮短。

(9) **at (one's)(sweet)will:** just as one chooses or pleases. 隨意。

He came *at* his own sweet *will*. 他由於自己願意來就來了。

(10) **eye-filling:** visually attractive; appealing to the eyes.

非常好看的。

The *eye-filling* exhibitions at the Palace Museum attract many tourists.

故宮博物院琳琅滿目的展覽吸引了很多觀光客。

(11) **full-course meal:** a complete, satisfying meal, consisting of three or more courses. 全餐。

(12) **first-run:** 參看範文3,注11。

(13) **plush:** luxurious. 豪華的。

怎樣寫好 英文 作文

評釋：

對於題目的正確了解非常重要。在動筆之前，先把題目仔細看一看，想一想。這篇作文的題目是The Fascination of a Large Department Store,其中最重要的一個字是fascination（吸引人、或使人著迷的力量或事物）。因此作者必須就一家大百貨公司的這一方面的優點加以描述。

在這篇作文裡面，重點都放在 fascination 上面。每一段講百貨公司的一個使人著迷的特點，並且在每一段裡都提到題目所說的fascination，但是不能總是重覆使用fascination這個字，必須想出幾個同義字或能產生同樣效果的字。在第一段裡，把百貨公司比喻為wonderland;第二段說 we cannot help but be fascinated by ... ；第三段使用 fascination;第四段使用 attractiveness;第五段使用 attractions。最末一段說 there is no more fascinating place than a large department store。

練 習 六

A. 根據本課內容，用完整的句子回答下列各問題：

1. What fascinating items can be found in the handicraft department of a large department store?

2. What can be found in the housewares department?

3. What other items can we find for sale on one floor of the department store?

4. Why is the atmosphere not experienced elsewhere?

5. Why doesn't the prospective buyer have to hurry?

6. What else can one do in a department store besides shopping?

7. What does a large department store mean to many of us?

B. 將下列各句譯成英文，儘量使用本課所學過的成語：

1. 朋友送他一張籃球比賽的票，他不能不去。

2. 這一章增加這本書的價值。

3. 我們不得不去參加宴會。

4. 我非常欣賞這本小說，竟致完全忘記時間過多久了。

5. 大體說來，我認為這是一個公平的決定。

C. 任選一題，作短文一篇：

1. The Excitements of Downtown

2. Shop Windows

II.說明文(Expository Essays)

5. Swimming

By nature, almost all animals and many birds know how to swim, even those that are not accustomed to[1] the water. Human beings, however, have to learn or be taught how to swim though it is said that the children of the natives on Orchid Island and some South Sea islands can often swim before they can walk.

Learning to swim should be an important part of one's education, especially in modern times when there is so much more travel than formerly. Sometimes an airplane is forced to come down in the ocean, and those who can swim have a better chance of surviving than those who can't. Similarly in a boating accident, many people have avoided drowning because they know how to swim to shore or float in the water and wait for someone to rescue them. And then there is the danger of being caught in a flood, or of falling into a pool or a lake accidentally. Not only may still in swimming result in[2] the saving of one's own life, but in the rescuing of others who are in danger of [3] drowning.

It is not very difficult to learn to swim. One must have confidence, and not be afraid of [4] letting his head go under the water occasionally. Some swimming instructors first show their pupils how to float, which is quite easy: one simply lies flat on the surface of the water, head well back, with the ears just beneath the water and the arms stretched out. Once the pupil is confident that he can always keep his head above the water and breathe, he soon learns the various strokes[5] and is able to move through the water easily. A story is told of a fisherman who one night fell overboard[6] in the Taiwan straits. He was given up[7] for lost, but was picked

五、游泳

差不多所有的動物和許多種鳥都天生就會游泳，即使那些不習慣於水的動物和鳥，也是如此。可是，人就必須學習，或者有人教，才會游泳，不過據說蘭嶼和若干太平洋島嶼的土著孩子，常在能走路之前，先會游泳。

學習游泳應該是教育當中的一個重要部分，尤其是在現代，旅行的機會要比過去多得多。有時候，飛機被迫降落在海洋上面，會游泳的人的生存機會，就多於不會游泳的人。同樣地，在划船遇難的時候，許多人之所以未淹死，只因為他們能夠游到岸上去，或在水上漂浮著，等別人來把他們救起。此外，我們有時還會遭遇水災，或者意外地掉落到一個池塘或湖裡面。游泳的技能不但可以保全自己的性命，而且還可以拯救其他可能淹死的人們。

學游泳並不很困難。你必須有信心，而且不要怕把頭偶而伸進水中。有些游泳教師先教學生在水上漂浮，這很容易：你只須在水面上平躺著，頭往後仰，耳朵進入水中一點點，胳臂伸出去。一旦學生確信他始終能使頭停留在水面之上，並且能夠呼吸，他很快就可以學會各種泳式，能在水中輕易地行進。據說，有一名漁夫在台灣海峽從船上掉落到海裡了。大家都認為他沒有生還的希望了，但是九小時後，他卻被另一艘船救起來了，在那九小時當中，他一直略感舒服地仰臥著在水面上漂浮著。他甚至宣稱他曾經睡了一會兒

up by another ship nine hours later. He had floated more or less comfortably on his back all the time. He even claimed to have slept for a while!

Not many of us probably desire to be champion swimmers. We are satisfied if we can dive into the water from a boat and swim for enjoyment or exercise. Yet perhaps we know at the same time that our ability to swim is an important skill in time of danger. It may enable us to save a life——maybe even our own! It is worth while[8], therefore, learning to swim.

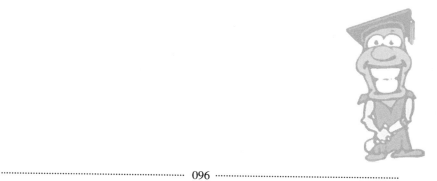

覺！

　　大概我們當中沒有很多人想得到游泳冠軍。如果我們能從小船跳到水裡，純然為了消遣或運動而游泳，我們就覺得滿足了。可是，同時我們或許也知道會游泳在遭遇危險時是一項重要的技能。它可以使我們拯救一條性命——說不定就是我們自己的性命。因此，學習游泳是很值得的。

注解：

(1) **accustomed to:** used to. 習慣於。

He is *accustomed to* working hard. 他習慣於努力工作。

I'll never get *accustomed to* this cold weather.

我難以習慣於這種寒冷的天氣。

(2) **result in:** have as a result; cause. 造成。

Drinking while driving *results in* many bad accidents.

開車的時候喝酒造成了許多嚴重的車禍。

His patient research *resulted in* the discovery of a cure for the

rare disease.

他的耐心研究終於發現了一種對此一罕見疾病的治療方法。

(3) **be in danger of:** 有…的危險。

He was *in danger of* losing his life. 他有喪失性命的危險。

The building is *in danger of* collapsing.

那棟房子有倒塌的危險。

(4) **be afraid of:** be full of fear about: be frightened about. 害怕。

Don't *be afraid of* the dog. 不必害怕那條狗。

Are you *afraid of* ghosts? 你怕鬼嗎？

(5) **stroke:** a manner of swimming, esp. one of several styles such

as the crawl or butterfly. 泳式。

He is a *breaststroke* champion. 他是蛙式的冠軍。

(6) **fall overboard:** fall over the side of a boat into the water.
從船上掉到水

(7) **give up: a.** stop believing that someone can be saved, esp. from death. 不再認為某人可以得救(尤指從死亡中得救)；對…不抱希望。

The explorers were *given up* for dead.

咸信那些探險隊員已經死了。

Everyone——the doctors, the nurses, his own family——had *given* him *up*, when he surprised them all by suddenly taking a turn for the better.

醫生、護士、他的家人全都認為他沒有希望了，這時他的情況突然好轉，使他們大吃一驚。

b. admit one's defeat or inability to do something.

承認失敗或不能做某事；放棄。

(8) **worth while:** worth the time or effort spent. 值得。

All this fussing is hardly *worth while*.

這一切的紛擾根本不值得。

It will be well *worth* your *while* to consider this offer.

這項提議很值得你考慮。

注意：如寫成worth-while或worthwhile,則只能用於名詞之前，如：a worthwhile experience, a worth-while effort.

評釋：

第一段為引言，指出人類必須學習，才會游泳。

第二段說明會游泳的好處。

第三段說明如何學習游泳。

末段為結語，強調游泳值得學習。

練 習 七

A. 根據本課內容，用完整的句子回答下列各問題：

1. Who is it said can swim before they can walk?

2. Why is learning to swim especially important in modern times?

3. When an airplane is forced to come down in the ocean, what can those who are able to swim do?

4. How have many people avoided drowning in a boating accident?

5. What may skill in swimming result in?

6. How can one learn to swim?

7. Why is it worth while learning to swim?

B. 將下列各句譯成英文，儘量使用本課學過的成語：

1. 到那裡去是不值得的。

2. 當你習慣的時候，辦公室的工作會是很容易的。

3. 他的疏忽造成了一個嚴重的錯誤。

4. 他的船有沉沒的危險。

5. 我恐怕傷了她的感情。

C. 任選一題，作短文一篇：

1. Hiking

2. A Bookshop

6. Why I Would like to Be Rich

The *Bible* states that be love of money is the root of all evil. It is possible, however, to be rich without letting riches become an evil. In fact, wealth, under certain circumstances, can be a blessing.

I would like to be rich if only because I could give away[1] money. People say that charity begins at home,[2] and I think my greatest pleasure would be to see that my father and mother had enough money to prevent their ever having to[3] worry again. I would also help my brothers and sisters, and some of my cousins to have a good start[4] in life.

Then I would like to be able to help many excellent charities such as the Free China Relief Association and the Kind Hearts Fund. I would also like to build a new hospital for our town and to contribute to making our country stronger by giving generously to the National Defense Fund. It would also give me great pleasure to see the happy looks on the faces of classical music buffs[5] when I donated to our talented, but financially troubled, city orchestra.

I would also like to be rich because I like expensive things, although I hope I would show good taste in what I buy. I would like a beautiful modern house standing in its own park, with fine gardens and a swimming pool. I would decorate the interior of the house with the best from the finest shops in Taipei. It would be simple but elegant, and I would entertain my friends there whenever I could.

Plenty of money also gives one an opportunity for travel. I have always wanted to travel, not only to educate myself but also[6] for the simple pleasure of satisfying my curiosity. I would fly throughout the countries of Asia and see Hong Kong, Malaysia, and Singapore to see

六、我為什麼願意富有

聖經上說愛財是萬惡之源。可是,一個人可以富有而不使財富成為禍害。實際上,在某些情形之下,財富可以成為一種福祉。

單憑我可以把金錢隨意贈送給別人,我就願意富有。俗語說,慈善要從家庭開始,我想我富有之後的最大快樂,是看到我的父親和母親都有足夠的金錢,以後永遠不必再發愁了。我也要幫助我的兄弟姐妹,和堂、表兄弟姐妹當中的幾位,給他們開創事業的奧援。

然後,我願意自己有能力幫助許多優良的慈善機關,如大陸災胞救濟總會和愛心基金之類。我也願意為本城建立一所新的醫院,並且大量捐助國防基金,以求對於保持國家強大的工作有所貢獻。我要捐款給本城那個隊員都天賦很高而經費支絀的管弦樂隊。當我看到那些古典音樂迷的面容上面的愉快神情時,我會感到很大的快樂。

我願意富有,也因為我喜歡昂貴的東西,不過我希望自己在買東西的時候,能夠顯示出高雅的趣味。我願意有一座漂亮的新式的房屋,坐落在它自己的庭園裡面,附有精美的花園和游泳池。我將用從台北最好的商店買到的最好的東西,來裝潢房屋的內部。這所房屋將是樸素而雅致的;每有機會,我就要在那裡款待朋友。

擁有大量金錢也能使我有機會出去旅行。我一直想要到各處旅行,不僅是為了教育自己,也是為了獲得滿足好奇心的單純樂趣。現在我要乘飛機遍遊亞洲各國,並且遊覽香港、馬來西亞和新加坡,親自體驗在海外的我國同胞的各種生活方式。我要去接受歐洲

firsthand the varied lifestyles of my fellow countrymen. I would expose myself to[7] the cultures of Europe and I would see the Americans as they really are. I would also see the place I have always wanted to visit——Disneyland.

Apart from [8] the prestige which richness brings—and I certainly would enjoy it after my present humble existence—I would take great delight in[9] giving people unexpected joy. I would go some nights into the poorer sections of the city, for instance, and give a needy person an NT$1000 bill; for whether he spent it on a hearty [10] meal or some new clothes, the look on his face would give me a warm feeling for days.

Perhaps one day I will be rich; if fate decrees it, I hope that I will be able to do everything I have just proposed.

文化的薰陶，看一看美國人的實際情況，並且到我一起想去的狄斯尼樂園玩玩。

除了財富為我帶來的顯赫之外(在經過目前這種卑微的生活之後，我當然會為這種顯赫而高興)，我也將很樂於給予旁人一些出乎意料的快樂。例如：我將在晚上前往城中比較貧苦的人們居住的地區，送給貧困的人一張千元大鈔；不論他拿這些錢去大吃一頓，還是買了一些新衣服，他臉上的神情都會使我心裡快慰好幾天。

也許有一天我會富有；如果命運注定那樣的話，我希望我把上面提出的事情一一做到。

注解：

(1) **give away:** give free of charge, not expecting anything in return.
贈送。

The old man *gave away* his entire fortune and went to live on a small island.

那位老人把他的全部財產送人，去一個小島居住。

(2) **Charity begins at home:** (proverb) A person's first duty is to help the members of his own family.

（諺語）慈善要從家庭開始（一個人的首要任務是照看自己的家人）。

(3) **have to:** 參看範文 3，注 1。

(4) **start:** a chance, opportunity, aid, or encouragement given to one starting on a course or career.

開始事業的機緣或助力。

(5) **buff:** a person very interested in and knowledgeable about the stated subject.

對某事特別有興趣或豐富知識之人。

Thousands of film *buffs* gather in France every year for the Cannes Film Festival.

每年有成千的影迷聚集在法國，看坎城影展。

(6) **not only... but also:** both... and.

不但…而且；…和…都。

He was *not only* tired, *but also* hungry. 他不但累，而且餓。

Not only men *but also* women take part in it.

男的和女的都參加了。

(7) **expose... to:** place... in a position likely to receive; lay open to.

使暴露於…之中；使遭受。

The young child was *exposed to* bad influences.

這孩子受到了壞的影響。

(8) **apart from :** in addition to; besides. 除…以外。

Apart from other considerations, time is a factor.

除了別人的顧慮以外，時間也是一個需要考慮的因素。

Our greatest foe, *apart from* indifference, is ignorance.

除了漠不關心以外，無知也是我們的大敵。

(9) **take delight in:** find pleasure in. 以…為樂。

He *takes* great *delight in* proving his classmate wrong.

他深以找出班上同學的錯為樂。

The barber *took* great *delight in* cutting the youth's long hair.

理髮師把那年輕人的長頭髮剪短感到很開心。

(10) **hearty:** substantial; abundant; nourishing. 豐富的；豐盛的。

I usually eat a light lunch and a *hearty* dinner.

我通常吃少量的午餐和豐盛的晚餐。

評釋：

這是一篇說明文。作者可以就這個題目說明他自己的想法。

注意 being rich 和 why I would like to be rich 的不同。這個題目是要你說明理由，所以不必就 being rich 多所發揮。

本文每段說明一個理由，而且每段的第一句都是一個主題句。第二段——I would like to be rich because I could give away money; 第三段——Then I would like to be able to help many excellent charities; 第四段——I would like to be rich because I like expensive things; 第五段——plenty of money gives one an opportunity for travel; 第六段——I would take great delight in giving people unexpected joy.

練 習 八

A. 根據本課內容，用完整的句子回答下列各問題：

1. What is the root of all evil?

2. How would the writer help his family if he were rich?

3. What charities would the writer help if he were rich?

4. What would the writer buy if he were rich?

5. What countries and place would the writer travel to if he were rich?

6. What would the writer take great delight in if he were rich?

B. 將下列各句譯成英文，儘量利用本課學過的成語：

1. 除費用問題外，時間也太遲了。

2. 他喜好繪畫。

3. 他不但對人親切，而且對動物也親切。

4. 他使自己面臨很大的危險。

5. 他把所有的錢都贈送給別人了。

6. 他的父親幫助他開創事業。

C. 任選一題，作短文一篇：

1. Why I Like My School (or Do Not Like my School)

2. If I Had One Million N. T. Dollars

7.　The Disadvantages of Being Young

"Schooldays are the best days of our lives" we are constantly being told—but is this true?

It certainly is not so when we examine the disadvantages of being young. In the first place[1], for many of us the old proverb that "children should be seen and not heard"[2] still applies. For example, when we put forth[3] an opinion on some topic our elders often reply that we are too young to[4] understand. This is particularly irritating when the topic concerns ourselves or our personal happiness; then we are treated not like the cute children that we are, but like soldiers in the army.

It is especially a disadvantage to be young when we are the youngest member of a family. If Father of Mother is in a bad mood then the eldest child first feels its effect; he gives vent to[5] his feelings on the next child, and so on in order of family precedence[6]. Whenever Father makes a concession, the youngest is the last to receive any of its privileges; whenever a gift is presented to the family, he is the last to view it firsthand. In fact, the only precedence the 'enjoys' is being first in the order of succession to bed.

In matters of amusement, our parents seem to know better than we what we enjoy. If there is an exciting kungfu movie playing at the local theater, our parents will certainly prohibit us from[7] seeing it. If there is a good horror story on television, the order "Off to bed!" is issued. And if some interesting gossip is being talked about in the living room, we are suddenly told to go and do our homework.

Another disadvantage of being young is that we are unreasonably

七、年幼的壞處

我們時常聽人說，「求學時期是我們一生當中最好的時期」——但是實際上真是如此嗎？

如果我們把年幼的壞處檢討一下，我們可以斷然說實際並非如此。第一，「孩子在長輩面前要保持緘默，如果長輩沒跟他們說話，他們不可先開口。」對我們當中的很多人來說，這句古老的諺語仍然適用。比方說，我們對某項問題提出意見時，長輩常回答說我們年紀太小，還不了解這個問題。如果談論的主題有關我們自己或我們個人的幸福，這種情形尤其氣人；在那個時候，我們的父母不按照實際情形把我們當成聰穎的兒童看待，而把我們視為軍隊中的士兵。

如果我們是家中最小的一份子，年幼對於自己尤其不利。如果父親或母親心情不好，最大的孩子首先感受到影響；他再把下一個孩子當成出氣筒，就這樣按照長幼的順序一個一個地發作下去。每當父親做了什麼讓步的時候，最小的孩子是最後得到惠益的人；每當家裡收到一件禮物的時候，總是最後才輪到他直接觀看那個禮物。實際上，他所「享受」到唯一的優先機會，乃是晚上要第一個上床睡覺。

在娛樂的事情方面，父母似乎比我們自己更知道我們喜歡什麼。如果當地的戲院放映一部很富於刺激性的功夫片，父母必定不許我們去看。如果電視上有一個很好的恐怖性節目，他們就會發出命令：「去睡覺吧！」如果大人正在客廳裡閒談一件有趣的事情，他們就會突然叫我們做功課去。

年幼的另一個壞處，是我們在錢財方面受到父母的不合理限

restricted by our parents in financial matters. They seem to think that younger we are, the[8] less need of money we have. Just the opposite is true! To prove this, we have only to [9] quote a list of items we still need—a bicycle, a basketball, a tape recorder, stereo equipment, camping gear, new clothes, and so on.

There are so many disadvantages of being young that only a few may be listed in such a short space, but mention must be made of[10] how much we are slighted by shopkeepers, of how much we are in demand for running errands [11] and doing household chores, and for being employed in such distasteful tasks as taking the garbage out in the worst of weather.

Indeed, we are a downtrodden [12] generation, and I for one [13] will be glad when I am an adult.

制。他們似乎以為越是幼小，對於金錢的需要越少。實際的情形剛好相反！為了證明這種情形，我們只須舉出我們仍然需要的一些物品——自行車、籃球、錄音機、音響、露營用具、新衣服，等等。

　　年幼的壞處太多了，因為篇幅所限，我只能舉出幾點，但是我一定還要提到小商人是如何的輕視我們，父母多麼常常需要我們跑腿，做家中的雜事，並從事諸如在最惡劣的天氣中把垃圾拿到外面之類的討厭工作。

　　的確，我們是被踐踏的一代，就我個人來說，我希望自己早日長大成人。

怎樣寫好 英文 作文

注解：

(1) **in the first place:** first in order; firstly (place: single step or stage in an arguement, etc.) 第一；首先。

(2) **Children should be seen and not heard:** Children should be silent in the presence of their elders and not speak until they are spoken to.

孩子在長輩面前要保持緘默，如果長輩沒跟他們講話，他們不可先開口。

(3) **put forth:** present; propose. 提出。

He *put forth* several suggestions for improving customer service.

他提出幾點建議，以求改善對顧客的服務。

(4) **too... to:** 參看範文 2，注 3。

(5) **give vent to:** allow free expression to (one's feelings). 發洩。

She *gave vent to* her feelings in sobs and tears.

她以啜泣和眼淚發洩自己的感情。

He is apt to *give vent to* his feelings.

他動不動就發火。

(6) **in order of precedence:** according to the right to a priority, or to a senior place. 按照優先的順序；按照長幼的順序。

The officials were seated *in order of precedence.*

那些官員按階級高低的順序入座。

(7)　**prohibit... from :** 禁止。

Students are *prohibited from* smoking in school.

學校裡禁止學生抽煙。

(8)　**the... the:** used before an adjective or adverb in the superlative degree to indicate that two things increase in a parallel way, or that one increases in a degree equal to that by which the other decreases. 越…越…。

The higher the ground, *the* cooler the air. 地勢越高，越涼快。

The sooner *the* better. 越快越好。

The more he has, *the* more he wants.

他得到的越多，越想再多得到一些。

(9)　**have only to:** 只須。

You have only to come—it's not necessary to bring anything.

你只要來就好了——不需要帶任何東西。

(10)　**make mention of :** speak of; refer to. 提到；談到。

He *made* no *mention of* your request. 他並沒有提到你的要求。

(11)　**run errands**: perform minor tasks (for others).

（為旁人）跑腿或做雜事。

The porter *runs errands* for the teachers. 門房替老師們跑腿。

(12)　**downtrodden:** treated badly by those in positions of power.

被壓制的；被蹂躪的。

(13)　**for one:** personally. 就個人來說。

I, *for one*, cannot agree. 就個人來說，我不能同意。

評釋：

作這種題目，要先仔細想一想，然後直截了當地說出自己的想法。對於大人當然可以稍加批評，但是說話要有分寸。有時可以開開玩笑，但是要避免流於尖刻諷刺。

本文內容是有計劃的，每段講述年幼的一個主要的不利情況。作者對於大人有所批評，但是語氣間帶有詼諧意味，使大人讀了覺得有趣，而不致心裡不舒服。

作者是最後說他們是被蹂躪的一代，你真的相信嗎？

練 習 九

A. 根據本課內容，用完整的句子回答下列各問題：

1. Why does the old proverb that "children should be seen and not heard" still apply?

2. What will happen if the writer's father or mother is in a bad mood?

3. What will happen whenever the writer's father makes a concession?

4. What will happen whenever a gift is presented to the family?

5. What is the only precedence the write 'enjoys'?

6. In matters of amusement, what do our parents seem to know better than we?

7. In financial matters, what do our parents seem to think?

8. What other disadvantages of being young does the writer mention?

B. 將下列各句譯成英文，盡量使用本課所學過的成語：

1. 他越有錢，花得越多。

2. 我們爬得越高，空氣越冷。

3. 他提出一項新理論。

4. 他發洩他的憤怒。

5. 他們被禁止在人行道（sidewalk）上騎自行車。

6. 他沒有提到這個事實。

C. 任選一題，作短文一篇：

1. The Pains and Pleasures of Growing up

2. Customs That Should Be Abolished

8. Holidays

" All work and no play makes Jack a dull boy "[1] runs[2] the proverb, and it is true that unless we have an occasional break from our daily routine, our health and our work will suffer as a result.

The way in which people spend their holidays varies greatly. During the summer, the majority travel to the seaside almost as a matter of course[3]. We have all experienced the excitement of planning for a day at the beach and of having our first glimpse of the ocean. We have all felt the healthful sun on our backs as we either bathe in its rays on the beach or play in the cooling ocean water. We shall never forget the hours spent in building sandcastles, in tossing Frisbees, and in playing beach ball[4] together. There are so many things to do during a day at the beach, though unfortunately the sun does not always meet[5] our expectation.

The more energetic people, and perhaps those with simpler tastes, prefer to spend their holidays hiking. Careful preparation is needed, for the inexperienced hiker easily falls victim to[6] insect bites or foot and skin soreness, unless he wears appropriate clothing. Most of them return, however, looking refreshed from the close encounter with nature.

Camping in tents attracts both young and old. Some prefer the convenience of pitching tent in designated campsites, while others prefer roughing it[7] in the wilderness. In either case, some experience in outdoor survival is necessary, if one is to prevent an unavoidable mishap from ruining an entire holiday.

The way people spend their holidays is as diverse as the people themselves. Some people go sailing in their own or in hired boats. Some people, more hardy, try the hazards of mountaineering. Others go exploring

八、度假

俗語說，「整天工作不休閒，會使孩子變成呆鈍沉悶」；我們天天從事日常的例行事務，如果不能偶而休息一下，結果必然會使自己的健康和工作受到不良影響。

人們度假的方式有很大的不同。在夏天，大多數人前往海濱，好像是例行的事情一般。計劃到海濱玩一天，第一次看見海洋，大家都有過這種興奮的經驗。我們或在海灘上做日光浴，或在涼爽的海水中嬉戲，都曾感受到曬在背上的有益健康的陽光。我們永遠不會忘記那些消磨於一起建造沙堡、投擲飛盤、和玩海灘球的快樂時光。在海濱玩一天，可做的事情太多了，只可惜陽光不能總是符合我們的期望。

那些精力更為充沛的人，和趣味更為單純的人，喜歡假日去徒步旅行。這種旅行需要很細心的準備，因為無經驗的徒步者很容易被蟲子咬，或者腳痛和皮膚痛，除非穿著適當的衣服。可是，大多數人在回來的時候，都由於同大自然密切接觸而顯得精神煥發。

在帳篷裡露營是一種老少咸宜的活動。有些人為了方便，喜歡在指定的露營地架起帳篷，其他的人們則喜歡在荒野過簡單的生活。在這兩種情形中，都需要有一些戶外求生的經驗，以防無可避免的不幸事件破壞了這次整個的度假。

度假的方式種類繁多，因人而異。有些人乘坐自己的或租來的小艇去航行。有些身體更為強壯的人們嘗試登山的冒險。另外一些人到一些迄今無法抵達的地方從事探險工作；還有一些人只是待在

in hitherto inaccessible places, while still others simply stay home saying that a rest is as good a change, which it sometimes is.

No matter [8] how we decide to spend our holiday, we must always keep in mind [9] that proper planning and preparation is the key to having a good time.[10]

家裡，他們認為一動不如一靜，這個話有時也很對。

　　不論我們決定怎樣度假，都必須時時牢記心頭，如果想玩得痛快，必須有適當的計算和準備。

注解：

(1) **All work and no play makes Jack a dull boy:** In the training of children, work and play should be intermingled.

在訓練兒童時，功課與遊戲應該並重。

(2) **run:** to be written, expressed, etc. in a specified way.

以某種方式寫成，說出等的。

How does the next verse *run*? 下一節詩是怎麼寫的？

The story *runs* like this. …據說…

(3) **a matter of course:** a natural or usual event; the usual way.

當然之事；自然之事。

You needn't ask him to come; he will come as *a matter of course*.

你不必要他來，他自然會來的。

It was *a matter of course* for Steve to go to Chengkungling after graduation.

史提夫畢業後去成功嶺乃當然之事。

(4) **beach ball:** a large inflated ball for playing with at the teach.

海灘球。

(5) **meet:** satisfy (needs, obligations, demands, etc.). 滿足；符合。

Does this *meet* your hopes? 這能滿足你的希望嗎？

This new road *meets* a long-felt need.

這條新的道路滿足了久已感到的需要。

(6) **fall victim to:** suffer because of (an action, etc.); become a sacrifice to. 因…而受害；成為…的犧牲品。

Take care not to *fall victim to* your own desires.

千成不要成為欲望的犧牲品。

Old Chang *fell victim to* the polluted air.

老張成了空氣污染的犧牲者。

He has recently *fallen victim to* opium.他最近染上鴉片煙癮。

(7) **rough it:** live in a simple and not a very comfortable way; live or sleep under hard or uncomfortable conditions, esp. outdoors. 過簡單而不舒適的生活；生活於艱苦或不舒適的狀況中，尤指在戶外。

Scouts like to *rough it* in the woods on weekend hikes.

童子軍周末健行是喜歡在樹林裡過簡陋的生活。

When I went abroad to study, I didn't have much money and had to *rough it* for a time.

我在國外讀書時錢不多，有一段時間不得不過簡樸的生活。

(8) **no matter:** it makes no difference.

Don't trust him, *no matter* what he says or does.

無論他說什麼或做什麼，都不要相信他。

No matter where you go, I'll be with you.

無論你去什麼地方我都要跟你在一起。

怎樣寫好英文作文

(9) **keep in mind:** bear in mind; constantly remember; not forget.

記住；不要忘記。

Please *keep* me *in mind* just in case you should have a job opening.

萬一有工作機會，請別忘了我。

Keep in mind your duty to our country.

記住你對國家應盡的責任。

(10) **have a good time:** enjoy oneself; pass a period of time pleasantly.過得很快樂。

Did you *have a good time* at the party last night?

你昨天晚上在派對中玩得快樂嗎?

We *had a good time* at the zoo today.

我們今天在動物園玩得很開心。

評釋：

本文以一句諺語開頭，說明度假的重要。

第二、三、四段分別說明到海濱去、徒步旅行和露營這三種最普通的度假方式。第五段說明其他幾種度假方式。

末段為結語，特別指出計劃和準備工作的重要。

練 習 十

A. 根據本課內容，用完整的句子回答下列各問題：

1. What will happen if we don't have an occasional break from our daily routine?

2. Where do the majority travel during the summer?

3. How do the more energetic people spend their holidays?

4. Why is careful preparation needed by the inexperienced hiker?

5. Where do some people prefer pitching tent?

6. How do others spend their holidays?

7. What is the key to having a good time?

B. 將下列各句譯成英文，儘量使用本課學過的成語：

1. 吃過早飯我就刷牙，這是當然之事。

2. 這個賭徒為自己的惡習（vice）而受害。

3. 時時要把我的忠告記在心頭。

4. 這個不符合我的要求。

5. 不論你去那裡，我都將和你在一起。

C. 任選一題，作短文一篇：

1. Sundays

2. Money

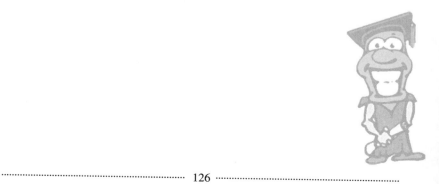

9. Inventions Which Are Needed

There is a saying that today's luxuries tomorrow's necessities. It is usually an invention that illustrates the truth of this, for progress is inevitable with the human race.

Inventions which are needed come easily to mind[1] when we think of [2] our comfort and convenience. We need a special shoe that has a layer of compressed air inside on which our foot will never tire over the longest journey. We need a cheap flying machine which we can put on[3] like a skin diver's [4] air tank to save us the necessity of walking at all. Perhaps moving pavements will be the best answer of all! We need a liquid which has only to be spread over the beard to remove it. And we certainly need an invention that will bring sunshine or rain as we desire, the only difficulty being that when we want sun for a picnic, others may want rain to water their fields or gardens.

There are also many electronic inventions which we need. We especially want a machine that will not only compute figures but write compositions for us! We can imagine what the high school student will think of [5] this. We want a machine that will translate foreign languages and which at the push of a button will give us the answer to any question we care to ask. Thus instead of hours of book learning we will learn to be good mechanics or good button-pushers!

The best inventions would be those which could cure illnesses and do away with [6] disease. Thus there is an urgent need for the invention of some machine that can diagnose early forms of cancer and similar diseases, in the same way that a car's engine is tested. There is a need for some form of pill or elixir which can cure the common cold, not just

九、我們所需要的發明物

有一句俗語說，現在的奢侈品就是將來的必需品。這句話的至理，往往可以由一項發明物來說明，因為人類的進步是無可避免的。

當我們考慮自己的安適和方便的時候，馬上就會想到我們所需要的一些發明物。我們需要一種特殊的鞋，裡面有一層壓縮空氣，兩隻腳穿上這種鞋，走最長的途程也永遠不會疲倦。我們需要一種廉價飛機，可以像潛水游泳者的氧氣筒一樣地戴起來，使得我們完全不必走路了。也許自動人行道是最好的辦法吧！我們需要一種液體，只要塗在鬍子上面，鬍子就掉了。當然我們也需要一種發明物，能在我們需要晴天的時候就帶來晴天，需要下雨的時候就帶來雨，唯一的困難是大家的需要未必一致，也許在我們想出去野餐需要晴天的時候，旁人也許需要雨水澆他們的田地或花園。

也有許多電子發明物是我們所需要的。我們特別需要一種機器，它不但能為我們計算數字，還能為我們作文！我們可以想像得到高中學生對於這個東西會有怎樣的想法。我們想有一種機器，它能翻譯外國語文，而且一按電鈕，就能為我們想要詢問的任何問題提供解答。因此我們可以不必整天念書，只要學習做一名優秀的技工或一名優秀的按電鈕的人就可以了。

最好的發明物是那些能夠治好病症和消除疾病的東西。因此，目前最迫切需要的發明物是一種能診斷早期癌症和其他類似病症的機器，其效能就像試驗汽車引擎一般。我們需要一種可以治好感冒的藥丸或仙丹，不僅是減輕它的徵候而已。我們也的確需要發明一

alleviate its symptoms. And there is a definite need for the invention of a device which will help the blind to " see " by means of [7] radar, and for an artificial voice for the dumb.

More fancifully, there is need for a truth detector. How much this invention would alter our lives! We would never deceive and never be deceived. How international relations would be affected! There would be no ulterior motives[8] at council tables, and government officials on the take[9] would all but[10] disappear. How much indeed would our own lives be altered if we could hear the truth about ourselves from an impartial machine!

So fast is the pace of modern progress that we can safely say no invention dreamed of today is beyond possibility of perfection tomorrow.

種能使盲人藉著雷達而「看見」的東西，和一種能使啞巴發出人造聲音的東西。

從一種更富於幻想的觀點來說，我們需要一種測驗真話機。這種發明物對於我們的生活將會造成多麼大的改變！我們將永遠不會欺騙旁人，也不會受旁人欺騙。國際關係將受到多麼大的影響！會議桌上將不會再有隱秘的動機，受賄的政府官員會幾乎完全絕跡。如果我們能從一架大公無私的機器聽到關於我們自己的實話，我們的生活將會有多麼大的改變！

現代進步的步調非常迅速，我們可以很有把握的說，我們現在所夢想的任何發明物，都可能在將來完成。

注解：

(1) **come to mind:** occur to one; be thought about.

被想到；被想起。(參看範文1，注 2 leap to mind)

A solution to the problem *came to mind* as I was listening to the radio.

我們在聽收音機的時候想出了解決這個問題的方法。

(2) **think of:** have in one's mind; consider; take into account. 考慮。

Do be careful—*think of* your poor mother!

千萬要小心——想想你可憐的母親！

We'd love to go traveling this summer, but *think of* the cost!

我們很想今年夏天去旅行，又不得不考慮費用的問題！

(3) **put on:** to cover (part of) the body with (something, esp. clothing) ; wear or place (something) on the body. 穿；戴。

She *put on* her hat and coat and went shopping.

她戴上帽子，穿上大衣，出去買東西。

Jane *put on* too much make-up. 珍擦了太多的化妝品。

(4) **skin diver:** one who engages in the sport or activity of underwater swimming using breathing apparatus.（使用呼吸器械的）潛水者。

(5) **think of:** have a certain opinion of; regard in a particular way.

對…持有某種意見或看法。

The critics did not *think* much *of* the book.

批評家對該書的評價並不高。

She doesn't *think* very highly *of* me.

她並沒有把我放在眼裡。

(6) **do away with:** put an end to; abolish. 廢除；消除。

The teachers want to *do away with* cheating in their school.

教師想消除校內作弊的風氣。

(7) **by means of:** by using; with the help of. 藉著；用。

By means of monthly payments, more and more people can afford to buy a car.

藉著按月付款的辦法買得起汽車的人越來越多了。

(8) **ulterior motive:** a hidden reason or intention, esp. a bad one. 隱密的（尤指不良的）動機。

Jack had an *ulterior motive* for visiting his uncle. He wanted to borrow some money from him.

傑克去看他的叔叔別有用心，他想跟他叔叔借錢。

(9) **on the take:** accepting bribes. 受賄。

The official was accused of being *on the take*.

那位官員被控受賄。

(10) **all but:** almost; nearly. 幾乎；差不多。

He is *all but* a king.

他簡直就是國王（有國王之權勢，只差無國王之名義）。

The speeding driver *all but* had an accident.

那個開快車的駕駛員幾乎出車禍。

怎樣寫好 英文 作文

評釋：

　　這個題目的寫作，需要運用想像力。你可以採取很認真的態度，也可以略帶詼諧的意味，或者和本文的作者一樣，兼用這兩種手法。

　　除首段為引言，末段為結語外，第二段講述有關舒適和便利的發明物，第三段講述電子發明物，第四段講述醫藥方面的發明物，第五段講述更富於幻想成分的發明物。

練 習 十 一

A. 根據本課內容，用完整的句子回答下列各問題。

1. What does an invention usually illustrate?

2. What inventions come easily to mind when we think of our comfort and convenience?

3. What electronic inventions do we need?

4. What would the best inventions be?

5. How would a truth detector change our lives?

6. How fast is the pace of modern progress?

B. 將下列各句譯成英文，儘量利用本課學過的成語：

1. 她差不多七歲了。

2. 他戴上眼鏡看報。

3. 我們用文字表達思想。

4. 在許多西方國家，死刑（death penalty）都已廢除了。

5. 老闆（boss）不太重視我的工作。（用think of）

C. 任選一題，作短文一篇：

1. My Ideal House

2. Things That Should Not Have Been Invented

10. The Companionship of Books

A man may usually be known by the books he reads as well as[1] by the company he keeps[2], for there is a companionship of books as well as of men.

A good book may by among the best of friends. It is the same today as it always has been, and it will never change. It is the most patient and cheerful of companions. It does not turn its back upon[3] us in times of adversity or distress. It always receives us with the same kindness: amusing instructing us in youth, and comforting and consoling us in age.

Books possess an essence of immortality. They are by far [4] the most lasting products of human effort. Temples and statues decay, but books survive. Time does not alter great thoughts, which are as fresh today as[5] when they first passed through their author's minds ages ago. What was then said and thought still speaks to us as vividly as ever from the printed page. The only effect of time has been to sift out [6] the bad products; for nothing in literature can long survive without being really good.

Books introduce us into the best society; they bring us into the presence of the greatest minds that have ever lived. We hear what they said and did; we see them as if they were really alive; we sympathize with them, enjoy with them, grieve with them; their experience becomes ours, and we feel as if we were in some way actors with them in the scenes which they describe.

Great men and their ideas never die. Preserved in books, their spirits live on[7]. The book is a living voice, to which one still listens. Hence we remain under the influence of the great men of old. The superior intellects of the world are as much alive now as they were ages ago.

十、與書籍為友

　　我們可從一個人結交的朋友，知道他的為人，也可以從他所讀的書，知道他的為人，因為我們不僅可以與人為友，也可以與書為友。

　　一本好書可以成為我們最好的朋友。它過去怎樣，現在仍是怎樣，而且將來永遠不會改變。它是一個最有耐心而愉快的友伴。在我們遭遇逆境和困苦的時候，它不會不理我們。它永遠以同樣的親切態度來接待我們：在青年時期，愉悅和教導我們，在老年時期，慰藉我們。

　　書籍具有一種不朽的本質。它們是人類努力的一種最持久的產物。廟宇和雕像不免頹毀，但是書籍永遠存在。時間不會改變偉大的思想，在今天，那些偉大思想仍然像許多年前它們湧現在作者心靈之中的時候同樣新鮮。作者當年所說的話和所想的事情，現在仍然像過去同樣生動地從印刷的篇幅傳送到我們心靈之中。時間對於書籍的唯一作用，是把不好的作品加以淘汰；因為在文學的園地之中，除非真正美好的作品，絕對不能長久存在。

　　書籍引導我們和最優秀的人士晤聚；書籍把我們帶到那些最偉大的曠世的才智之士的面前。我們傾聽他們所說的話和所做的事情；我們看見他們，好像他們真的活在世上一般；我們和他們發生同感，與他們同享樂，共憂苦；他們的經驗成了我們的經驗，我們覺得自己彷彿就是在他們所描述的一幕一幕戲劇當中和他們共同表演的演員。

　　偉大的人物和他們的觀念永遠不死。他們的精神都保藏在書裡，繼續活下去。書是活人的聲音，我們仍然要聆聽。因此我們仍然處於昔日偉大的影響之下。世界上那些卓越的有才智的人們，現在仍然像很久以前一樣地活在世上。

A good book, like a good friend, is really a rare treasure which no one should ever be without.

好書像好朋友一樣，是每個人都不可缺少的稀罕珍寶。

注解：

(1) **as well as:** as much as; as truly as; in addition to.

除…外；不懂；又；和 。

He has experience *as well as* knowledge.

他既有學問，又有經驗。

We will travel by night *as well as* by day. 他將日夜兼程。

The child is active *as well as* healthy.

這孩子不但健康，而且活躍。

(2) **the company he keeps:** 有一句俗話說：A man is known by the company he keeps.

從一個人所交往的朋友，可以知道他的為人。

注意：keep a person company=be or go with him

(3) **turn (one's) back (up) on:** to refuse to take any notice of or give support to (a person, organization, etc.).

不理睬；不支持。

He never *turned* his *back on* his neighbors when they needed help.

鄰居需要幫助時，他從不會不予支援。

(4) **by far:** in a great degree; very much.

很；極（用作比較級和最高級形容詞之加強語）。

Henry is *by far* the best athlete in the school.

亨利是校中首屈一指的運動員。

(5) **as... as:** 和…一樣。

Sue is *as* tall *as* Jane. 蘇跟珍一樣高。

Kaohsiung is not *as* large *as* Taipei. 高雄沒有臺北大。

(6) **sift out:** to separate or get rid of after closely examining.
找出；汰除。

The judge *sifted out* the truth from the conflicting testimony.

法官從相反的證詞中找出事實。

(7) **live on:** survive; endure. 繼續活著；持久。

Although he died over a hundred years ago, his name continues
to *live on*.

雖然他已經在一百多年以前去世，他的名字仍繼續存在。

His spirit *lives on* in all our hearts.

他的精神仍存活在我們的心裡。

評釋：

第一段為引言。

第二、三、四、五段分別就書的一個方面加以說明，每段的第一句都是主題句。末段為結語。

練 習 十 二

A. 根據本課內容，用完整的句子回答下列各問題：

1. How may a good book be among the best of friends?

2. Why do books possess an essence of immortality?

3. What has been the only effect of time on books?

4. How do books introduce us to the best society?

5. Why do great men and their ideas never die?

6. Why is a good book like a good friend?

B. 將下列各句譯成英文，儘量利用本課學過的成語：

1. 我們的木瓜樹長得和房屋一樣高。

2. 電視的影響力比電影大得多。（用by far和比較級形容詞）

3. 他不理睬我了。

4. 他給我忠告，又給我金錢。

C. 任選一題，作短文一篇：

1. The Pleasures of Reading

2. My Favorite Book

11. People Who Live Dangerously

Some people thrive on[1] peril. They are the ones who regard a normal life as a bore.

Stunt men[2] live dangerously. They are usually employed by film studios to do daring deeds which will excite movie audience. The cost of life insurance for such people must be enormous, for they face accident and even death several times a day. Thus, when the hero's car is forced off the road by the villain's and goes flying over a cliff, it is not Steve McQueen[3] or Roger Moore[4] who emerges from the wreckage, but some unfortunate " stand-in "[5] who specializes in the work. Although such people are well paid, many confess that it is the thrill of living dangerously that compels them to be professional stunt men.

Others who pursue a dangerous career are circus performers, such as acrobats[6] and animal tamers. We cannot but[7] admire the trapeze artist[8] working so skillfully at dizzying heights, or those who put their heads in lions' mouths, or those who swallow a mouthful of fire. They not only do their work brilliantly but[9] seem to enjoy every dangerous minute of it. They would no doubt find even such a glamorous position as a ring master[10] dull and unappealing by comparison.

Explorers, whether they go up mountains, penetrate jungles, or rocket into space, are living dangerously. Although the purpose of their travels is often for some higher[11] goal, explorers readily admit that they enjoy the element of danger in what they do. Parachutists, deep sea divers, and race car drivers—no matter[12] they are professionals or amateurs—all fall into the same category.

Most people probably never think must about the danger of their

十一、過危險生活的人們

有些人靠著危險而發達。他們是那些認為正常生活令人厭煩的人。

電影裡面的替身過著危險的生活。他們通常被電影製片廠雇用，做出那些使電影觀眾驚心動魄的冒險行為。這種人的人壽保險費數額一定是巨大的，因為他們每天都數次面臨意外事故，甚或死亡。因此，當主角的汽車被暴徒的車逼迫離開道路，頭朝下從懸崖跌落下去的時候，從破毀的車子裡出來的並不是史提夫‧麥昆或羅傑‧摩爾，而是專門從事這種工作的可憐的「替身」。這些人的待遇顯然都很優厚，但是許多人承認，驅使他們作職業替身的乃是危險生活的刺激。

其他從事危險生涯的人們還是馬戲班演員，如空中飛人、走繩索者和馴獸者之類。對於那些在令人暈眩的高空做出巧妙表演的高空飛人，那些把腦袋伸進獅子嘴裡的人們，那些吞下一口火的人們，我們不能不加以讚賞。他們不僅把自己的工作做得很出色，而且似乎從充滿危險的每時每刻獲得樂趣。無疑地，他們會認為甚至像馬戲班指揮表演者那樣富於刺激的職位，相形之下也是安靜而乏味的。

那些探險者，不論他們是上山，深入叢林，或乘火箭進入太空，都是過著危險生活的人。雖然他們的目的常是為了達成某項崇高的目標，他們都欣然承認自己從所做之事的危險成分中得到樂趣。跳傘者、深海潛水者、和跑車駕駛人，不論他們是專業人員，還是業餘的從事者，都屬於這一類人。

大多數人對於自己工作當中的危險性質，也許從來不曾多加思

work and do it only because it suits them better than any other activity. Think for a moment of the danger that coal miners meet underground, and consider the policemen and the firefighters who risk their lives everyday to protect our own. And don't forget such humble workers as window washers on tall buildings and street cleaners on busy streets. Such people never seem overly concerned about the dangers they face.

What is it that makes men and women live dangerously? It is probably something deep down in the human race which inspires us to conquer the unknown and to take delight[13] in seeking adventure.

索,他們之所以從事那項工作,只因為它比任何其他活動更為適合他們。想一想礦工在地下所面臨的危險,想一想警察和消防隊員每天為了保護我們的生命而冒著他們自己生命的危險。也不要忘記那些諸如在高樓上清洗窗戶者和熱鬧街道上的清道夫之類卑微的工人們。這些人似乎從來不為自己所面臨的危險而過分憂慮。

是什麼動機促使男人和女人去過危險生活呢?大概在人類的心靈深處有一種東西,激使我們去征服未知的事物,並且以冒險為樂事。

注解：

(1) **thrive on:** grow strong or prosper by taking or using(something).

由於取得或使用（某種東西）而茁壯或興旺。

This is the style of life *on* which he seems to *thrive*.

他似乎是靠著這種生活方式興旺起來的。

That famous model *thrives on* compliments.

那個著名的模特兒因為受到讚揚而興旺起來。

(2) **stunt man:** a substitute who replaces an actor in scenes requiring hazardous or acrobatic feats. 替身。

(3) **Steve McQueen:** (1930-1980)award-winning American movie actor.

史提夫‧麥昆(獲奧斯卡金像獎之美國電影演員)。

(4) **Roger Moore：**(1928-)British movie actor famous for his role as 007.

羅傑‧摩爾(以演 007 出名之英國演員)。

(5) **stand-in**=stunt man.

(6) **acrobat:** person who can do clever things with his body, such as balancing on a rope. 賣藝者（如走繩索者之類）。

(7) **cannot but:** cannot avoid; must. 不得不。

I *cannot but* admire your decision. 我不得不欽佩你的決定。

(8) **trapeze artist:** 表演空中飛人的馬戲班演員。

(9) **not only... but:** 參看範文 6，注 6。

(10)	**ring master:** a person who directs performances in a circus. 指揮馬戲表演之人。

(11)	**high:** morally or spiritually exalted; noble; virtuous. 高尚的。

Dr. Sun Yat-sen is man of *high* character.

國父孫中山先生是個品格高尚的人。

Writing is a *high* calling.寫作是一個高尚的職業。

He has *high* aims and hopes to become a nuclear physicist.

他懷有高尚的目標和希望，要做核子物理學家。

(12)	**no matter:** 參看範文8，注8。

(13)	**take delight in:** 參看範文6，注9。

評釋：

第一段是引言，第二、三、四、五段各就一種過危險生活的人加以敘述。這是一種很自然的安排。大多數作文的人遇到這種題目都會這樣作的。末段就過危險生活者的動機加以探索。

練 習 十 三

A. 根據本課內容，用完整的句子回答下列各問題：

1. What are stunt men employed to do?

2. Why must the cost of life insurance for stunt men be enormous?

3. What compels such people to be professional stunt men?

4. How do acrobats and animal tamers pursue a dangerous career?

5. What do explorers readily admit?

6. Why don't most people probably ever think about the danger of their work?

7. What is it that makes men and women live dangerously?

B. 將下列各句譯成英文，儘量利用本課學過的成語：

1. 所有的人都因為享有自由而生活得很好。

2. 這位律師不得不表示異議（disagree）。

3. 我父親極喜好在星期天釣魚。

4. 不論你要到城裡的什麼地方去，隨時都可以叫到計程車把你送到那裡。

C. 任選一題，作短文一篇：

1. The Appeal of Danger
2. People I Dislike Very Much

12. Science and the Housewife

In the past several decades science has completely revolutionized the life of the average housewife.

Perhaps it is in the kitchen that the most marked develop ments are to be seen. Gone are the iron pots and pans which used to take hours of hard scrubbing to clean; in their place, new scientific methods have given us stainless steel and aluminum utensils. Another development is the manufacture of liquid detergents and cleansing powders to keep the kitchen—and everything in it—spotless.

Electricity has brought the most change and given the greatest benefit to the housewife. No longer[1] does she have to labor over a wood-burning stove; she can now cook her meals in a microwave oven. Nor does she have to worry about food spoiling anymore, for refrigerators prevent this. Smoke and cooking odors are channeled outside by exhaust fans, rice is steamed in rice cookers, and toast is prepared in toasters—all of wich are powered by electricity.

Scientific developments have also improved the bathroom. Large, comfortable bathtubs with hot running water at one's disposal[2] make taking a bath[3] an absolute pleasure. The ceramic industry has provided beautiful and easy-to-clean patterned tiles for both floors and walls.

Scientific progress has also left its mark in the rest of the house. New fabrics are now used to make elegant curtains and plastic blinds[4] which keep our fire-proof rugs from[5] fading. Light and easy-to-use vacuum cleaners make housework a less burdensome task. And plastic paints in every color imaginable, or wallpaper of any design, can help to create any atmosphere desired.

十二、科學與主婦

在過去幾十年當中，科學已經完全革新了一般家庭主婦的生活。

最顯著的進展，也許可以從廚房看得出來。過去的那種鐵製的鍋和平鍋，需要用力擦洗好幾個小時才能乾淨，現在都不見了，代之以新的科學方法提供給我們的不銹鋼和鋁製的器皿。另一種發展是，液體清潔劑和去污粉的製造可以使廚房——和廚房裡面的一切——一塵不染。

電為家庭主婦帶來最多的變化，和最大的福祉。她不必再在燒木柴的爐子前面辛苦工作了；現在她可以用微波烤箱做飯。她也不必再擔心食物會腐壞，因為有電冰箱保藏食物。抽風機把煙和做菜的氣味排送到外面去，用電鍋蒸米飯，用烤麵包機烤麵包——所有這些東西都是用電力推動的。

科學的發展也使浴室大有改進。舒適的大澡盆，再加上隨時都有的熱水，使入浴成為一種真正的樂事。製陶工業提供美觀而容易清洗的花瓷磚，鋪地面和牆壁都可使用。

在家庭的其他方面，科學的進步也留下了痕跡。現在各種新的織物被用來製成雅致的窗簾和塑膠百葉窗，使我們的防火地毯可以保持本來的顏色。很輕而容易操作的真空吸塵器使得做家事不像從前那樣累人。具備各種顏色的塑膠漆，和圖樣繁多的壁紙，可以為房間製造一種你所希望有的任何氣氛。

怎樣寫好 英文 作文

The stereo[6], tape recorder, television, and radio must not be forgotten in discussing the benefits of science to the housewife. These forms of entertainment certainly help her to relax between household chores or at the end of the day. The transistor radio is especially helpful in making the work of the modern housewife seem less monotonous.

In many respects we may say that science is the handmaid of the housewife.

　在討論科學為家庭主婦所帶來的福祉的時候,我們不可忘記音響、錄音機、電視和收音機。這些娛樂一定會幫助她在一件一件的家庭雜務之間,或一天快過完的時候,輕鬆一下。電晶體收音機特別有助於使現代家庭主婦的工作比較不單調。

　在許多方面,我們都可以說科學是家庭主婦的婢女。

注解：

(1) **no longer:** 參看範文1，注7。

(2) **at one's disposal:** 參看範文3，注20。

(3) **take a bath:** wash (oneself) in a bathtrb.

洗澡；沐浴（指在澡盆裡洗澡，淋浴則是take a shower）。

(4) **blinds:** something that obstructs vision or keeps out light, as a window shade, venetian blind, etc.

窗簾；百葉窗。

(5) **keep... from:** prevent... from (happening or doing).

防止；阻止。

I mustn't *keep* you *from* your work. 我不能讓你耽誤工作。

(6) **stereo:** 參看範文1，注11。

評釋：

做這種題目，最好先想出五、六個主要的項目，並舉出例證。

第二段說明科學在廚房裡面造成的變化。第三段說明電為家庭主婦帶來的福祉。第四段說明浴室裡面的變化。第五段說明科學在家庭的其他方面所發生的影響。第六段說明科學為家庭主婦帶來的休閒時的享受。

第一段是開頭，只有一句話，說科學革新了家庭主婦的生活，第七段是結尾，也只有一句話，和第一段相呼應，說在許多方面，科學已經成了家庭主婦的婢女。

練 習 十 四

A. 根據本課內容，用完整的句子回答下列各問題：

1. What has science done to the life of the average housewife?
2. Where are the most marked developments to be seen?
3. What have new scientific methods given us in place of iron pots and pans?
4. What is another development which can be seen in the kitchen?
5. What has brought the most change and given the greatest benefit to the housewife?
6. How have scientific developments also improved the bathroom?
7. What can help to create any atmosphere desired?

8. What things can help the housewife to relax between chores or at the end of the day?

B. 將下列各句譯成英文，儘量利用本課學過的成語：

1. 她不再是一個美麗的年輕女人了。

2. 群眾使那個賊無法跑掉。

3. 我們現在有充分的人力可供我們任意的使用，足可迅速完成這項工作。

4. 我姐姐每次洗澡要洗一個鐘頭。

C. 任選一題，作短文一篇：

1. Modern Transportation

2. When the Electricity Stops

13.   Where There's a Will There's a Way[1]

Necessity is said to be the mother of invention: if it is so, then will is certainly the father.

The power of the human will is immense. It is of such force that nothing can stand against[2] it. When a man is determined to do something, obstacles serve to strengthen his resolution, opposition becomes an aid to accomplishment, and setbacks turn into[3] acts of renewed conviction.

The truth of this is quite obvious when we see how men first improved upon[4] their condition. From damp caves to high-rise apartments is not a long time compared with the history of the earth. The stride from kindling to atomic power, from a candle to an electric lamp is gigantic in terms of [5] human determination to overcome the difficulties that confronted man in the earliest times.

We need not only look to the past for evidence, but we may also look at ourselves today. We can think of [6] many people who started life[7] without a dime and who are now millionaires; we may point to the many men and women without a formal education who are now leading executives in large corporations; we may also point to many a humble inventor whose name has become a household word[8] — all because he was determined to find a way to reach his goal.

We may also think of our friends to see how their will has shown the way. There are many people who, though not so gifted as others, have by sheer diligence surpassed their more brilliant fellows. Success is more often a result of hard work than of genius, and oftentimes the person who excels others is the one who fails five times and succeeds at the sixth.

It is strange, moreover, how often those who succeed fail in their

十三、有志者事竟成

據說需要為發明之母；如果這個話說得不錯，意志必然是發明之父。

人類意志的能力是巨大的。它擁有非常強大的力量，任何東西都不能和它對抗。當一個人決心要做某件事的時候，障礙可以加強他的決心，反對變為成就的助力，挫折化為再度充滿信念的行為。

如果我們看一看人類最初如何改善自己的狀況，便可以十分明顯地看出這番道理的真實性。同地球歷史比起來，從潮濕的洞穴發展到多層的公寓並沒有經過一段很長的時期。從人類克服最早期所面臨的困難的決心來看，從開始使用火到原子動力，從蠟燭到電燈，可以說是邁了極大的一步。

我們不僅要從過去尋找證明，也可以看一看今天我們自己的情形。我們可以想起許多人，開始創業時都是一文不名，現在卻已成了百萬富翁；我們可以指出很多男人和女人，他們沒有受過正式教育，現在卻已成為領導群倫的大公司主管人員；我們也可以指出許多卑微的發明家，現在在工業界已經成為家喻戶曉的人物——完全因為他下定決心想辦法完成自己的目標。

我們也可以想一想自己的朋友們，看看他們如何在意志的驅策之下，努力奮鬥。有許多人，雖然天資不如別人，卻全憑勤勉而勝過了那些更有才華的儕輩。成功多半是辛勤努力的收穫，而非天才的成果，出類拔萃的人常常是失敗五次在第六次成功的人。

而且，說起來很奇怪，那些成功的人最初往往遭遇多次失敗。

initial efforts. In this respect we can think of the moral that Robert Bruce[9] learned from the spider. And we should never forget the example set[10] by Dr. Sun Yat-sen, who succeeded in overthrowing the Manchu Dynasty only after suffering repeated setbacks.[11]

Yet this proverb holds true[12] not only in the material world but also in the world of ideas. Let us reflect on the determination of the early Christians who faced death and torture to propagate their faith, of the philosophers who faced public disgrace to further their ideas, of the Chinese patriots who rose against[13] foreign rule —all of whom overcame immense obstacles by perseverance and an unshakeable belief in a higher goal.

No matter[14] how often we may face failure, we should always bear in mind the truth of this age-old saying.

在這一方面，我們可以想到布魯斯從蜘蛛獲得的教訓。我們永遠不要忘記　國父孫中山先生所留下的榜樣，他經過多次挫折之後，終於推翻滿清。

可是，這個諺語不僅適用於物質的世界，也適用於觀念的世界。讓我們想一想那些不惜面對死亡和磨難來傳播他們的信仰的早期基督徒，不惜面對公眾的貶抑來宣揚自己的思想的哲學家，以及那些反抗異族統治的中國志士──所有這些人都憑著堅持不懈和對於一個崇高目標的信心而克服了巨大的障礙。

我們無論遭遇多少次失敗，都應該時時牢記這句古老名言的真諦。

注解：

(1) **Where there is a will there is a way:**(proverb)If one has the determination to do something, a way of doing it will be found. （諺語）有志者事竟成。

(2) **stand against:** oppose steadfastly; resist.

堅決反對；和⋯對抗。

Who can *stand against* destiny? 誰能對抗命運?

His father *stood against* corruption. 他父親反對貪污腐敗。

(3) **turn into:** be changed, transformed, or converted into. 變成

He has *turned into* a very pleasant fellow.

他變成了一個和藹可親的人。

When it freezes water *turns into* ice. 水能結凍成冰。

(4) **improve upon(or on):**produce something better than.

改善；改進。

You complexion is wonderful; don't try to *improve upon* nature.

你的膚色非常好，不要設法改變天生的膚色。

This can hardly be *improved on*. 這無法改進。

(5) **in terms of:** with respect to; in relation to; especially about.

以⋯的觀點來看；就⋯來說。

He tends to think of everything *in terms* of money.

他總會以錢的觀點來衡量一切。

In terms of mileage, this car gets 35 miles per gallon.

就哩數來說，這部汽車每加侖汽油可以跑三十五哩。

(6) **think of:** call to mind; remember; recall. 想起；記起。

Can you *think of* what he looked like? 你記得他的長相嗎？

(7) **start life:** begin one's career. 創業。

He *started life* as a door-to-door salesman.

他最初是個挨戶兜售的推銷員。

(8) **household word:** a well-known name or saying, etc.

家喻戶曉的名字或諺語等。

His name is a *household word* here, but is practically unknown abroad.

他的名字在此地家喻戶曉，在國外根本沒有人知道。

Sony has become a *household word* all over the world.

「新力」在世界各地成了家喻戶曉的名字。

(9) **Robert Bruce:**(1274-1329), a gallant Scottish king who spent most of his lift trying to free his country from English rule. A legend is told of Bruce hiding from his enemies. He was lying on a bed in a wretched hut. On the roof above him, Bruce saw a spider swinging by one of its threads. It was trying to swing itself from one beam to another. It tried six times and failed. Bruce realized that he had fought the same number of battles in vain against the English. He decided that if the spider tried a seventh time and succeeded, he also would try again. The

spider's seventh attempt was successful. Bruce took heart, and went forth to victory.

布魯斯（1274-1329）是一位英勇的蘇格蘭國王，一生大部分時間致力於把他的祖國從英國的統治解救出來。根據傳說，布魯斯躲避敵人時躺在一個破爛小屋的床上，看到上方屋頂上有個蜘蛛吊在一根蛛絲上擺來擺去，想從一根橫樑搖擺到另一根橫樑，一共搖擺了六次，結果都失敗了。布魯斯這才明白，他也跟英國打過同樣次數的仗，而且失敗了。他下定決心，如果那個蜘蛛再作第七次嘗試而且成功的話，他也要再度嘗試。那個蜘蛛的第七次嘗試果然成功了。布魯斯信心大增，乃邁向勝利之路。

(10)　**set an example:** be a model; act in a way that is worthy of imitation. 成為模範，樹立榜樣。。

You must *set an example* to the younger children.

你一定要做弟弟們的榜樣。

He quit smoking and *set a* good *example* to his colleagues.

他戒煙了，為同事們樹立了一個好榜樣。

(11)　**setback:** a reversal, hindrance, or interruption in progress or development. 挫折；挫敗。

He suffered a financial *setback.*

他遭到財務上的挫敗。

(12)　**hold true:** be regarded as true; continue to be true.

適用；有效。

It has always *held true* that man cannot live without laws.

人沒有法律就不能生存，這乃是一定不移的道理。

What I told you about Bill's lack of tact also *holds true* for his brother.

我跟你說過比爾不圓通，他的兄弟也是如此。

(13)　**rise against:** take up arms to fight against; revolt against.

反抗；反叛。

The people *rose against* the tyrant. 人民反抗暴君。

(14)　**no matter:** 參看範文8，注8。

評釋：

題目是一句諺語，最好先把這句諺語的意思解釋一下。

第一段為引言，把題目的含義解釋為決心或意志可以克服一切障礙。第二段說明意志力的強大。第三段把人的意志力同馴服自然的力量關聯起來。以後各段舉出一些實例，說明有決心的人如何終於獲得成功。末段為結語。

練 習 十 五

A.　根據本課內容，用完整的句子回答下列各問題：

1.　Why is the power of the human will immense?

2.　Why is the truth of this quite obvious when we see how men first improved upon their condition?

3.　What evidence of this truth can be found when we look at ourselves today?

4.　How has the will of our friends shown the way?

5.　What example was set by Dr. Sun Yat-sen?

6.　What can we reflect on in the world of ideas which shows that this proverb holds true?

B.　將下列各句譯成英文，儘量使用本課學過的成語：

1.　這項規則在一切情形下均屬有效。

2. 林肯堅決反對奴隸制度。

3. 可口可樂在中國也已經成了一個家喻戶曉的名字。

4. 我對於他的翻譯不能再加以改進。

5. 我一時想不起他的名字了。

6. 他留(wear)長頭髮，為他的弟弟樹立一個不良的榜樣。

C. 就下列格言任選一題，作短文一篇：

1. " The Pen Is Mightier Than The Sword."

2. " All That Glitters Is Not Gold."

14. The Attractions of Taiwan for Visitors from Abroad

In 1544 a hearty band of Portugese sailors set eyes on [1] a small island situated in the warm waters off the coast of mainland China and cried "Ilha Formosa"—or " Island Beautiful." This fitting description of Taiwan is still true today.

Most people who visit Taiwan are amazed at the harmonious blending of the traditional and the modern. Taipei in particular[2] is the mecca[3] of all lovers of traditional Chinese culture. Here they may see ornate temples wedged between towering office buildings, high-rise apartments overlooking tile-roofed houses, handicraft and bric-a-brac[4] stores side by side with ultra-modern department stores —all within a few square miles. Here they can have a glimpse of the history of the distant past in the Confucian Temple, built in memory of [5] China's most revered teacher and philosopher. They can also survey the history of days just past in the Dr. Sun Yat-sen Memorial Hall and the Chiang Kai-shek Memorial Park, which were built to commemorate Republican China's two greatest leaders.

Without a doubt, the premier attraction in the Taipei area for all sightseers —local or foreign —is the National Palace Museum. Housing over 250,000 Chinese art treasures spanning[6] the entire 5,000-year history of China, the museum displays only a small fraction of its collection at any one time. Even though exhibits are changed every three months, it has been estimated that it would take over ten years to display everything in storage.

Interesting sites outside of [7] Taipei also have an appeal for visitors

十四、台灣吸引海外遊客的事物

在西元一五四四年，一群精神飽滿的葡萄牙水手看到位於中國大陸海岸外的溫暖海洋中的一個小島，不禁高呼「美麗的島」。現在這個恰當的形容仍然適用。

大多數訪問台灣的人，對於這個地方的傳統與現代的協調的混合都感到驚奇。台北尤其是傳統中國文化的所有愛好者心目中的聖地。在這裡，他們可以看到金碧輝煌的廟宇夾在高聳的辦公大樓中間，多層的高樓公寓俯瞰瓦頂的房屋，手工藝品與小件古董的店鋪和極端現代化的百貨公司並排存在——都在幾平方哩的範圍之內。在這裡，他們可以在為紀念中國最受崇敬的教師和哲學家修建的孔廟看到久遠的歷史。他們也可以在國父紀念館和中正紀念堂看到近代的那段時期的歷史，二者都是為了紀念中華民國兩位最偉大的領袖而建造的。

無疑的，對所有國內或外國觀光客來說，台北地區最吸引人的地方是國立故宮博物院。該院收藏的藝術珍品達二十五萬件以上，那些作品的年代涵蓋了全部中國歷史；每次展出的藝術品只是其中的一小部分。雖然展覽品每三個月更換一次，據估計要用十年以上的時間，才能把全部收藏品展覽完畢。

台北以外的名勝，對於來自國外的遊客也很有吸引力。在台灣

from abroad. In northern Taiwan, Yeh Liu offers exciting views of the cliff, the sea, and the nearby fishing villages and beaches. It is a unique and frequently visited spot because of its reddish coral rock formations; many of these are shaped like animals and people and have been given fanciful names, such as Queen's Head, Cinderella's Shoe, and Dinosaur.

In central Taiwan, Mt. Ali has become the most beloved mountain retreat [8] on the island. It is indeed a beautiful area, full of cypress trees —some nearly 1500 years old —and thousands of cherry trees, whose blossoms dot the mountainside in spring. Other scenic spots in this part of the island include Sun Moon Lake, Pao Chueh Temple, and the Taroko Gorge. The last is a geological wonder with mile after mile of limestone and marble cliffs intersected by a well-paved highway. Early missionaries once remarked that the Taroko Gorge was comparable in grandeur to the Grand Canyon.

In southern Taiwan, the foreign visitor should definitely not miss the Kenting Tropical Park, The site abounds with[9] different trees and shrubs from various countries of Asia. Coral can also be found there, indicating that this area was once under the tea millions of years ago.

The people of Taiwan are perhaps the island's greatest attraction. The Chinese have been called the politest and friendliest people on earth, and nowhere else in the world can traditional Chinese culture be experienced by the foreigner than [10] on this bastion of freedom.

北部，野柳的懸崖、海面、以及附近的漁村和海灘提供了很使人興奮的景色。這個地方因為有那些淡紅色的珊瑚礁構成物，風景奇特，是遊人常去之所；那種構成物大多具有動物和人的形狀，人們為它們起了一些奇特的名字、如皇后頭、灰姑娘的鞋、和恐龍之頭。

在台灣中部，阿里山已經成為台灣最受喜愛的山中遊憩地。這的確是一個風景優美的地區，有很多柏樹，其中最老的已經生長了一千五百年之久；還有成千上萬株櫻樹，到了春天，櫻花點綴著山坡。在台灣的這一部分，其他的遊覽勝地還有日月潭、寶覺寺和太魯閣。太魯閣幽峽是一個地質學上的偉蹟，一哩接連一哩的石灰石和大理石的懸崖，由一條路面良好的公路貫穿其間。早期的傳教士們曾說太魯閣幽峽的壯麗可以媲美大峽谷。

在台灣南部，外國遊客一定不能不去墾丁公園。這裡有很多來自亞洲各國的各種樹和灌木。也有珊瑚，表示這個地區在幾百萬年以前曾經是在海底的。

這個島嶼上最能吸引遊客的也許是台灣的人民。中國人被稱為世界上最有禮貌最友善的民族，外國人在世界任何其他地方，都不能體驗到這個自由堡壘上這種傳統的中國文化。

注解：

(1) **set eyes on:** see; perceive; look at. 看。

From the moment I *set eyes on* that dress, I knew I would buy it.

我一看到那件衣服就知道我會買它。

(2) **in particular:** especially. 尤其；特別。

I noticed her eyes *in particular*, because they were so large.

我特別注意她的眼睛，因為它們很大。

(3) **mecca:**(from the name of Muhammad's birthplace)goal of one's ambitions; place one is anxious to visit.（出自回教教主穆罕默德的誕生地「麥加」）希望的目標；渴望前往的地方。

(4) **bric-a-brac:** bits of old furniture, china, ornaments, etc., esp. old and curious, of no great value. 小古董。

(5) **in memory of:** as a way of remembering or being reminded of (a worthy person, etc.) 紀念。

They erected a monument *in memory of* those killed in battle.

他們立碑紀念陣亡將士。

(6) **span:** extend, reach, or pass over (space or time).

遍及；涵蓋。

The child's interests *spanned* many subjects.

這孩子的愛好遍及各科。

His life *spanned* almost the whole of the 19th century.

他的壽命涵蓋了整個十九世紀。

(7) **outside of:** outside.在…的外面

His grave lay *outside of* Taipei. 他的墳墓在台北的城外。

(8) **retreat:** a place of refuge, seclusion, or privacy. 僻靜的地方。

The wealthy businessman has an apartment in Taipei and a *retreat* by the ocean.

這位富商在台北有一層公寓,在海濱有個僻靜的地方。

(9) **abound with (or in):** have in large numbers or great quantity. 有很多;富於。

Modern industry *abounds with* opportunities for young men and women with imagination.

現代的工業為富有想像力的青年男女提供了很多機會。

(10) **nowhere else... than:** at on other place... than.

除了…以外,在任何別的地方都不能。

Nowhere else in Taipei can you buy this kind of cake *than* at this store.

除了本店以外,這種餅在台北市任何地方都買不到。

評釋：

　　本文兼具說明文和描寫文的性質。重點要放在 attraction 這個字上面。

　　全篇的設計很明確，是按照一種很普遍的方式處理的；除了首段的引言之外，講到台北，故宮博物院，北部的野柳，中部名勝，南部名勝，和中國人。

　　當然也可以有其他的寫法，如強調指出中國的烹任，農村繁榮，經濟發展，十大建設等。這都看個人如何處理和取捨了。

練 習 十 六

A. 根據本課內容，用完整的句子回答下列各問題：

1. Where is Taiwan situated?

2. What are most people amazed at when they visit Taiwan?

3. What may visitors see in Taipei?

4. Why is the National Palace Museum the premier attraction in the Taipei area?

5. What views does Yeh Liu offer? Why is it a unique and frequently visited spot?

6. What are some scenic spots in central Taiwan?

7. What scenic spot in southern Taiwan shouldn't the visitor miss?

8. Why are the people of Taiwan the island's greatest attraction?

B. 將下列各句譯成英文，儘量使用本課學過的成語：

1. 這條河裡有很多魚。

2. 明天我沒有什麼特別要做的事情。

3. 她作一首詩紀念她的祖母。

4. 我一看到這位新鄰居，就愛上她（fall in love with）了。

C. 任選一題，作短文一篇：

1. What Visitors from Abroad Find Disappointing about Taiwan

2. Why I Find My Hometown Attractive (or Unattractive)

15.　The Post Office

There must surely be few [1] people today who have failed to notice at some time or other [2] a little green van speeding through the streets, or a young man dressed in green pedaling down a lane on his bicycle, or a pair of mailboxes along the roadside —one a bright red, other a dark green. These are the more frequent signs of an institution whose services are so widespread as to[3] affect a great deal of our everyday lives.

The post office is perhaps first thought of [4] in connection with[5] our letters. The collection and delivery of correspondence was, indeed, its first function, and now it handles millions of letters a month. We have all used the mailbox at the corner, and watched its contents being collected; we have perhaps seen these letters being sorted in the District Post Office; and the sight of the mailman bringing our mail (or going straight past our house) is surely a familiar one. Apart from[6] ordinary correspondence, the post office handles a steady stream of bulk mail, the vast rush of the Christmas greeting cards, thousands of parcels and packages of varying sizes, and a very large volume of domestic and foreign periodicals. To this must also be added the register and express services, the sending of surface mail to practically every free nation in the world, and finally, the complex system of air mail services.

Nowadays the post office offers a variety of banking services. We may safely mail money to anyone in Taiwan by using a postal money order. We may use the postal remittance service to buy the latest publications or the newest gadgets. If we wish to save our money instead, we can deposit it there: interest on savings is high, business hours are longer than those of a regular bank, and additional services —like the

十五、郵局

在目前這個時代，一定很少有人不曾在某個時候看到一輛綠色小貨車在大街上急駛而過，或一名綠衣青年騎著腳踏車從巷子裡走過，或路旁的兩座郵筒，一座是鮮紅色的，一座是深綠色的。這些就是一個服務非常普遍、對我們日常生活影響很大的機構的比較常見的標誌。

談到我們的信件，首先就會聯想到郵局。信件的收取和投遞的確是郵局的首要職責，現在郵局每月要處理幾百萬件信函。我們都往街角的郵筒裡面投過信，並且看到過裡面的信被取走；我們或許也曾看見過那些信件在支局裡面被揀選分類；郵差送來郵件(或從我們門前走過去)，也確是常見的景象。除了普通信件之外，郵局還處理源源而來的大宗投寄的印刷品郵件，大量湧來的聖誕卡，成千上萬件各種大小的包裹，和大量國內和國外的期刊。此外，我們還須談到掛號和快遞的服務，寄往世界所有自由國家的陸路和水路郵件的運送，以及航空郵件的複雜體系。

現在郵局還提供種種的銀行服務。我們可以用郵政匯票很穩妥地把錢寄給在台灣的任何人。我們可以利用郵政劃撥購買最新的出版物或最新的精巧小機械。如果我們想把錢儲蓄起來，我們可以把錢存在郵局：儲蓄存款利率很高，營業時間比銀行長，還有額外的服務，如代收水、電費等，使我們節省很多時間。

accepting of payment of our utility bills —help us to save much time.

One noteworthy aspect of the post office, of special interest to philatelists,[7] is the beautiful stamps it issues. New sets of stamps are usually issued to commemorate important occasions, such as New Year's or the anniversary of the passing of Dr. Sun Yat-sen. In conjunction with[8] the Chinese Cultural Renaissance Movement, the post office regularly issues stamps of reproductions of famous Chinese art works. Paintings and masterpieces of calligraphy, bronze, ceramics, jade, and tapestry found in the collection of the National Palace Museum provide topics for individual stamps and for sets. Such stamps have consistently received top honors at international stamp exhibitions.

Since its establishment in 1896, the Chinese Post Office has steadily grown in size and in importance, until now we should find our daily life very difficult indeed without its varied services. There is little[9] doubt that in the future it will develop even greater importance.

郵局還有一個值得注意的貢獻，為集郵者所特別關心的，就是它所發行的美麗的郵票。為了紀念重要的節日，如新年，國父逝世紀念日之類，通常會發行一套新郵票。為了配合推行中國文化復興運動，郵局經常發行複印著名藝術品的郵票。故宮博物院收藏物品中的畫、書法傑作、青銅藝術品、陶器、玉器和綴錦都為單張或成套的郵票提供題材。這些郵票經常在國際郵票展覽會中獲得最大的榮譽。

自從中國郵局在一八九六年成立以來，它在規模和重要性方面都一直在不斷地增長，現在如果沒有郵政的各種服務，我們會覺得日常生活甚為困難。郵局將來一定還會獲致更大的重要性。

注解：

(1) **few:** few 和 a few 的意義不同。few 的意義是 not many（不多；很少），常含否定意味；a few 的意義是（有一些）。

例如：

I have *few* books. 我沒有什麼書。

I have *a few* books. 我有幾本書。

(2) **at some time or other**: at some unspecified time. 在某個時候。

She'll visit him *at some time or other* during the spring vacation. 她將在春假的某個時候去看他。

(3) **so... as to:** …到…的程度；如此的…以致（在 so 的後面用形容詞或副詞，在 as 的後面用不定詞，說明結果。）

I wouldn't be *so* clumsy *as to* break the vase.

我不至於笨拙到打破那個花瓶。

Who could be *so* mean *as to* do a thing like that?

誰會卑鄙到去做那種事呢?

The windows are *so* small *as* not *to* admit much light.

那些窗戶非常小，光線進不了多少。

(4) **think of:** 參看範文 9，注 2。

(5) **in connection with:** with regard to. 關於。

The meeting is *in connection with* the proposal to build the new subway.

會議與興建新地下鐵路的建議有關。

(6)　**apart from:** as wall as. 除了…以外。

Apart from the cost of the sweater, the color doesn't suit me.

這件毛衣除了價錢以外，顏色也不適合我。

(7)　**philatelist:** a stamp collector. 集郵者。

(8)　**in conjunction with:** along with; together with. 會同；一同

The FBI is working *in conjunction with* the local police to recover the stolen art treasures.

聯邦調查局正會同當地警察尋找失竊的藝術珍品。

(9)　**little:** little和a little 意義不同。little的意義是not much（不多；很少），常含否定意味；a little 的意義是（有一些）。

例如：

There is *little* hope. 沒有什麼希望。

There is *a little* hope. 有一點希望。

評釋：

　　本文除首段為引言，末段為結語外，第二段較長，講述郵局的主要業務，第三段講述儲匯業務，第四段講述有關集郵的事情。

　　本文有一個特色，就是有些句子很長，包含一連串的片語和子句，如第一段的第一句，第二段的第三句和第四句，第三段的第四句等。

練 習 十 七

A.　根據本課內容，用完整的句子回答下列各問題：

1.　What have few people surely failed to notice at some time or other?

2.　Apart from ordinary correspondence, what else does the post office handle?

3.　What kinds of banking services does the post office offer?

4.　What are the topics of stamps which have consistently received top honors at international stamp exhibitions?

5.　What has happened since the establishment of the Chinese Post Office in 1896?

B.　將下列各句譯成英文，儘量利用本課學過的成語：

1.　他除了自己而外，從來不為任何旁人設想。

2. 瑪麗是如此的粗心大意，竟致忘記把書帶來。

3. 我們將會獲勝，這是沒有什麼可以懷疑的。

4. 沒有多少時間了。

5. 不要忙，你還有一點時間。

6. 沒什麼人知道這個。

7. 有幾個人知道這個。

C. 任選一題，作短文一篇：

1. The Train Station

2. The Library

16.　A Letter to a Pen Pal

No. 3, 4th Floor
Alley 24, Lane 84
Jen Ai Road, Section 3
Taipei, Taiwan
Republic of China
March 5, 1983

Dear Sue,

Thank you for your letter in which you stated you had passed your examination. May I heartily congratulate you.

I'm also happy to hear that your elder brother has been accepted into the Air Force. He should have some exciting stories to tell when he comes home on leave [1].

Did I tell you that my friend, Lilly, is going to be a secretary? She has been looking for [2] such a job for a long time, and last week she had an interview at a big exporting firm. They are going to make her the assistant manager's secretary and she's looking forward to [3] working there very much.

One day last week I visited the National Palace Museum to see a special exhibition of Sung Dynasty paintings. I especially enjoyed Fan K'uan's masterpiece. You know, he is considered to be one of the greatest Chinese landscape painters. His works reflect a realistic portrayal of nature and emphasize her immense vastness.

I am still struggling through Woody Allen's [4] *Side Effects*. I'm reading it on my own [5] to try and get a better understanding of American humor. I find it so strange that you Americans enjoy making so much fun

十六、致筆友的一封信

仁愛路三段八十四巷二十四弄三號四樓
中華民國台灣省台北市
一九八三年三月五日

親愛的蘇：

接讀來信，知你已通過考試。我要很熱誠地向你致賀。

得悉令兄已經進入空軍服役，我也很高興。將來他休假回家的時候，一定有一些使人興奮的故事對你們講。

我有沒有告訴你，我的朋友麗蕾就要去當秘書了?她一直在找這樣的一個工作，已經很久了，上星期她到一家很大的出口貿易公司面談。他們要她擔任襄理的秘書，她正很熱切地盼望著到那家公司工作。

在上星期，有一天我去國立故宮博物院，參觀宋朝名相的展覽。我特別喜歡范寬的傑作。你知道，他被認為是中國歷史上三大山水畫家之一。他的作品反映出對於自然的寫實的描繪，並且強調自然的浩大。

我還在苦讀艾倫的「副作用」。我是在憑自己的能力閱讀這本書，希望能對美國人的幽默有更深的了解。你們美國人那麼喜歡用死亡當作開玩笑的題材，我覺得很奇怪。對了，我向你推薦的林語

of [6] death. By the way[7], did you read Lin Yu-tang's *My Country and My People* that I recommended? It really is a good introduction to Chinese life and culture.

Last Saturday, Mother and I went shopping downtown together. I have been invited to a "housewarming party," and the main reason we went was to have a dress made [8] for me. A "housewarming party" in China means that people who move into a new house give a party to celebrate the occasion. My new dress is beautiful, though it cost an arm and a leg[9] to buy it. It is a Chinese-style *ch'i-pao* made of light blue silk with gold designs. I'll sent you a picture (with me in it, of course) in my next letter.

I've been going to shadow-boxing[10] classes every morning at sunrise. I feel healthier and more alert, and this kind of exercise helps to keep my figure slim.

How is your " romance" with David going? Are you still good friends after he disappointed you by forgetting your birthday? Paul and I went to the movies together last Sunday, so you can gather[11] that our relationship is progressing.

Well, that's all for now. Hoping to hear from you soon.

Your Friend

Mary

堂的「吾國與吾民」你讀了沒有?那部作品介紹中國人的生活和文化,寫得很好。

上星期六,母親和我到市中心區去買東西。我被邀請參加一個溫居宴。我們去買東西,主要理由是我想訂做一件新衣服。在中國,「溫居」的意思就是一家人遷入新屋,舉行宴會,慶祝一番。我做的新衣服很漂亮,雖然這件衣服花了我一大筆錢。那是一件中國式的旗袍,用淡藍色緞子做成的,上面帶有金色的花紋。下次信裡將寄給你一張照片 (當然,照片裡面有我)。

我每天早晨日出時去學太極拳。我覺得自己比以前更健康更靈活了,而且這類運動可以幫助我保持身材的苗條。

你同大衛的「羅曼史」進展如何?他那次忘記你的生日,使你很不高興,現在你們兩個還是很要好吧?保羅和我上星期日一起去看電影,你可推想得到我們的關係是在進展之中。

好了,不多寫了。盼早日惠覆。

你的朋友
瑪麗

注解：

(1) **on leave:** absent from duty (esp. in government service or in the military) with permission. 休假

The Chinese engineer went back to Taipei *on* a month's *leave*.

那個中國工程師休假一個月回台北了。

Private Chang will be *on leave* for one week before going to Kinmen.

士兵張去金門之前將有一星期的休假。

(2) **look for:** seek; search for. 尋找

I have lost my gloves. Will you help me *look for* them?

我把手套丟掉了。你幫我找一找好不好？

(3) **look forward to:** expect with hope or pleasure.

盼望；期待（後面接用動名詞或名詞）。

Larry is not *looking forward to* seeing the dentist.

賴瑞不想去看牙醫。

It's a shame I couldn't attend the baseball game. I was *looking forward to* seeing it so much.

真可惜，我不能去看這場棒球賽。我早就盼望著去看這場比賽。

(4) **Woody Allen:** (1935—)U.S. film comedian, screenwriter, director, and short story writer.

伍迪·艾倫（一九三五年生，美國電影喜劇演員、電影腳本

作者、導演及短篇小說作家）。

(5) **on one's own:** 獨自；自力。

(6) **make fun of:** joke about; laugh at; mock; ridicule .

嘲笑；取笑；開…的玩笑。

It is wrong to *make fun of* a cripple. 取笑殘廢的人是不對的。

Her classmates enjoy *making fun of* her curly hair.

班上同學很喜歡取笑她的鬈髮。

(7) **by the way:** in the course of one's remarks; incidentally.

還有；對了；順便說一說（說話的人忽然想到一件與本題無

關的事情，用以改變話題者）。

(8) **have... made(=have... made to order):** made, produced, or

manufactured upon receipt of the order and according to the

wishes of the customer. 訂做；訂製。

I'm *having* some bookshelves *made* for my study.

我要替我的書房訂做一些書架。

How much does it cost to *have* a box of name cards *made*?

印製一盒名片要多少錢？

(9) **cost an arm and a leg:** cost a large amount of money. 花很多錢。

Their new house must have *cost* them *an arm and a leg*.

他們這棟新房子一定花了很多錢。

(10) **shadow-boxing:** making the motions of attack and defense, as

in boxing, in the absence of an opponent.

與假想對手鬥拳；打太極拳。

191

(11) **gather:** learn or conclude from something said or done.

推測;猜想。

I *gather* Betty is ill, and that's why she hasn't come.

我想貝蒂大概是病了,所以沒有來。

What did you *gather* from his remarks?

你從他的談話猜想到什麼?

I didn't *gather* very much from his phone call.

我從他的電話猜不出什麼來。

評釋：

　　本篇提供書信的格式，以供參考。

　　我們以前對於作文所提出的寫作原則，也同樣用於寫信。

　　寫這種友誼性的信，筆調最好要親切自然。不妨用一些口語中常用的俗語，但是俚語仍以不用為宜。

練 習 十 八

A. 根據本課內容，用完整的句子回答下列各問題：

1. Why does Mary heartily congratulate Sue?

2. When should Sue's elder brother have some exciting stories to tell?

3. What kind of job did Mary's friend, Lilly, get?

4. What did Mary see when she visited the National Palace Museum?

5. Why is Mary reading Woody Allen's book?

6. Why did Mary recommend Lin Yu-tang's book to Sue?

7. Why did Mary and her mother go shopping downtown together last Saturday?

8. What has Mary been doing every morning?

9. Where did Paul and Mary go last Sunday?　What can Sue gather from this?

応用進階篇

B. 將下列各句譯成英文，儘量使用本課學過的成語：

1. 我在尋找我的筆。

2. 孩子們在盼望假期。

3. 他請假回美國了。

4. 他們在背後嘲笑他。

5. 他花一千元新台幣訂做了一雙皮靴。

C. 任選一題，寫一封英文信：

1. Write a letter to your cousin asking him (or her) to spend the summer (or winter) vacation with you, and saying what you will do together.

2. Write a letter to your elder brother (or sister) who is studying abroad.

194

III. 記敘文(Narrative Essays)

17. Typhoon

The television announced that super typhoon Betty had unexpectedly changed course. She was now poised[1] for a direct attack on Taipei.

Our family wasted no time in taking the necessary precautions.[2] Mother began filling the bathtub with water while Elder Sister went to the neighborhood grocery store to purchase some nonperishables[3], such as noodles and canned goods. Father collected the potted plants which decorated our front yard and stored[4] them in our small, enclosed back porch. He also climbed a bamboo ladder and took down our TV antenna, which blew away during last year's typhoon, and inspected our newly repaired roof tiles. Being the youngest member of the family. I was responsible for preparing the necessary candles and making sure[5] that our flashlight had fresh batteries. Whitey, our Pekingese, raced back and forth, his occasional barks sounding like commands ordering us to inspect his doghouse.

The full fury of the storm hit while we were enjoying our dinner. We were eating in the living room so that[6] we could hear the special news reports on the radio. It was during one of these reports that everything suddenly went black.

I turned on[7] the flashlight which I had prepared so that everyone could at least [8] place their rice bowls on the table (instead of misplacing them on the floor); then I got up[9] to light the candles I had strategically placed around the house. I reached[10] into my pocket for a pack of matches only to[11] discover it empty. " That's okay, son," Father said reassuringly, " Here, use my lighter."

十七、颱風

電視報告超級強烈颱風貝蒂已經出人意料地改變方向。現在她即將直接襲擊台北。

於是我們家趕快採取必要的防範措施。母親開始把浴盆放滿了水，姐姐則到附近的食品雜貨店購買不會很快腐壞的食物，如麵條和罐頭之類。父親把裝飾前院的盆栽花草集中起來，存放在那個很小的圍蔽起來的後門廊裡。他並且爬到竹梯子上面，把電視天線取下來，因為去年來颱風的時候天線被颳走了；他又把我們新修好的屋頂的瓦檢查一遍。因為是家裡最小的孩子，我負責準備必需的蠟燭，並弄確實使手電筒裡有新乾電池。我們的哈巴狗小白跑來跑去，偶而吠叫一聲，聽起來好像是吩咐我們檢查他的狗舍的命令。

我們正在吃晚飯的時候，颱風颳得最猛烈。我們在起居室裡吃飯，為的是可以聽到收音機的特別新聞報告。就在某一次報告特別新聞的時候，整個房屋都變成一片漆黑了。

我打開了我事先準備好的手電筒，以便大家至少可以把飯碗放在桌子上(而不是誤放在地板上)然後我站起來，要把我事先曾做戰略部署放置在室內各處的蠟燭燃起來。我伸手到衣服口袋裡面拿火柴，結果卻發現口袋是空的。「沒有關係，孩子，」父親叫我不要擔心，「來，用我的打火機點。」

After lighting the candles, we all seated ourselves once again at the dinner table to finish our meal, which by this time had become very cold. Mother re-warmed the hot-and-sour soup and we finished our meal to the sounds of howling wind and pouring rain.

No sooner had we cleared the table than[12] Elder Sister cried out: "There's someone trying to break in[13] the back door!" Father and I went to investigate, and to our great surprise, there was someone caught out in this ferocious weather seeking, it seemed, refuge in our house. Father unlocked and opened the door and a white mass of matted fur [14] darted into the living room. Poor, frightened Whitey ran under the sofa stayed there for the duration of the storm.

As Father fastened the door a resounding thud echoed through the house. A stream of thoughts flashed through my mind —the roof had collapsed, an earthquake had struck, the brick wall surrounding our house had been blown down.

Each family member rushed to a different window to see what had happened. And once again, it was Father's calm words which reassured us: " Everything is okay. One of our papaya trees was uprooted, that's all [15]."

We awoke early the next morning the inspect the damage. Our brick wall was still standing, and no windows had been broken. Only one tree had been downed, the large papaya. And it was now that we discovered how everything almost wasn't "okay" last night: the papaya tree had fallen directly on Whitey's doghouse, smashing it to pieces. But fortunately, "almost" doesn't count [16].

　　點好蠟燭之後，我們又在餐桌前面坐下來，繼續吃飯，這時飯菜已經涼了。母親把酸辣湯重新熱一熱，我們就在狂風咆哮和大雨傾盆聲中吃完了晚飯。

　　我們剛把飯桌清理好，姐姐就大聲喊叫：「有人要從後門闖進來!」父親和我去視察一下，使我們大感驚愕的是，我們發現有人陷在外面這種惡劣天氣之中，好像是要到我家裡避一避。父親開了鎖，打開門，一堆被水淋濕的纏結起來的白毛就衝到起居室裡面了。可憐的受驚的小白跑到沙發底下，在整個暴風雨期間，一直待在那裡。

　　當父親把後門關牢的時候，一個很響亮的重擊聲迴盪在整個房屋裡面。一連串的念頭閃現在我的心頭——屋頂坍下來了，地震了，房屋四周的磚牆被颳倒了。

　　家裡的每個人跑到一個不同的視窗，去看看究竟發生了什麼事情。又是父親的鎮靜使我們放心了：「一切都很好。我們的一棵木瓜樹被連根拔起了，如此而已。」

　　第二天早晨我們起得很早，去察看損害的情形。我們的磚牆還立在那裡，屋頂瓦沒有颳掉的，窗戶沒有打破的。只有一棵樹颳倒了，就是那棵大木瓜樹。現在我們才發現，昨晚一切幾乎不是「很好」的?木瓜樹正砸在小白的狗舍上面，把它壓得粉碎。但是，幸而「幾乎」是不算數的。

注解：

(1) **poised for:** in a state of readiness to act or move.

已準備好，即將採取某種行動。

The army was *poised for* action. 軍隊準備戰爭。

(2) **take precautions:** do something in order to avoid possible known danger, discomfort, etc. (precaution: a measure taken in advance to avert possible evil or to secure good results).

採取預防措施。

Precautions will be *taken* to guard against the recurrence of such an incident.

將採取預防措施以防止此類事件再度發生。

(3) **nonperishables:** articles or items, esp. of food, not subject to rapid spoilage. （通常用複數式）不會很快腐壞的東西(尤指食物)。

(4) **store:** put away for future use. 存放。

Mother *stored* her winter clothes at the dry cleaner's.

母親把冬天的衣服存放在乾洗店。

(5) **make sure:** 參看範文 2，注 7。

(6) **so that:** 參看範文 1，注 9。

(7) **turn on:** start the flow of (liquid, gas, electrical current, etc.) by turning a tap, pressing a switch, etc. 打開。

Turn the radio (lights, etc.) *on*. 把收音機（電燈等）打開。

注意：turn on 之相對語為turn off, 參看範文 2，注 17。

(8) **at least:** 至少。

It will cost *at least* twenty dollars. 至少要花二十塊錢。

You should write *at least* one composition a week.

你一個星期至少要寫一篇作文。

(9) **get up: a.** arise; stand up; get to one's feet. 站起來。

The old man fell down and had trouble *getting up*.

那老人跌倒後站不起來了。

b. get out of bed. 起床。

When do you usually *get up*? 你平常什麼時候起床？

(10) **reach:** stretch out the hand for some purpose. 伸手（拿東西）。

The clerk *reached* for a box of sugar. 店員伸手拿一盒糖。

She *reached* across the desk for her dictionary.

她把手伸過書桌去拿字典。

(11) **only to:** but in the end ; but with the result that.

only 後面接用不定詞，意思是：卻；結果卻；想不到。

John won a great deal of money, *only to* lose it all the next night.

約翰贏了很多錢，想不到第二天晚上又統統輸掉了。

She resolved one problem, *only to* face another.

她解決了一個難題，結果又遇到另外一個難題。

(12) **no sooner... than:** 參看範文 1，注 3。

(13) **break in** (also **break into**): force an entry (into); force one's way in (to). 闖入；強行或非法進入。

怎樣寫好 英文 作文

The firemen *broke in* the door of the burning house.

消防隊員破門進入著火的房屋。

(14) **matted fur:** twisted, ungroomed hair of an animal.

纏結在一起的獸毛（如被水淋濕時的情形）。

(15) **that's all:** and nothing else. 如此而已。

"I need five hundred dollars, dad, *that's all.*"

「爹，我需要五百塊錢，如此而已。」

(16) **doesn't count:**不算數(不在考慮範圍之內)。

The race *doesn't count* because he started before the gun sounded.

這次比賽不算，因為槍還沒響他就起跑了。

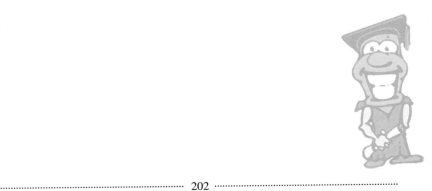

評釋：

第一段為引言，第二段講述一些預防措施。第三段講述颱風來襲和斷電，氣氛開始緊張。第四、五段講述如何應付並繼續吃飯。第六段出現新的緊張局面。第七段為緊張的高潮。第八段為緊張之消除。末段綜述災情。父親自始至終的鎮定態度，是貫串全文的一股暗流（undercurrent）.

練 習 十 九

A. 根據本課內容，用完整的句子回答下列各問題：

1. What had the television unexpectedly announced?

2. What precautions did the writer's family take?

3. When did the full fury of the storm hit?

4. What did the writer do when the typhoon hit?

5. What did everyone do after the candles were lit?

6. What happened when the writer's father unlocked and opened the door?

7. What happened as the writer's father fastened the door?

8. What did each family member do after hearing a resounding thud?

9. What did the family find when they inspected the damage?

B. 將下列各句譯成英文，盡量利用本課學過的成語：

1. 那裡至少有三十人。

2. 我明天要在六點鐘起床。

3. 請打開電視，以便我可以看新聞。

4. 我們應該預防意外事件。

5. 我們不在家時，竊賊曾經非法闖入。

6. 他整個下午都在等她的電話，結果卻發現他的電話壞了。

C. 任選一題，作短文一篇：

1. An Accident

2. Air Pollution

18.　An Autobiography

I was born in a middle-class neighborhood in Taipei on June 7, 1966. I have two brothers and two sisters, all of whom are younger than myself. As the eldest child in our family, I have always had the responsibility of looking after[1] my little brothers and sisters when my parents were elsewhere occupied. This was more often the rule than the exception.

Both of my parents lead relatively active lives. My father is the manager of a trading company and often travels, both to southern Taiwan and to other countries in Asia. My mother is a housewife, but only a part-time one. She often takes on[2] odd jobs like sewing garments for my uncle when his tailor shop gets too busy, or helps to cook meals at aunt's small restaurant whenever she becomes short-handed.

There was nothing particularly outstanding about my elementary school education. I was a rather ordinary student and received quite average grades, except in arithmetic. Far from being[3] another Einstein, I did, however, consistently receive the highest grades in my class in this subject.

In junior high school, I started to develop a keen interest in reading. I read everything: newspapers, magazines, Chinese novels, and translations of Western classics. Perceiving my fondness for the printed page, my parents allowed me to enrol in a three-month speedreading course. The skills I learned in this course have enabled me to greatly increase my reading ability.

In senior high school, my interest in reading naturally began to extend to the reading of English books. Having already learned the fundamentals of this language in junior high school, I began to devote

十八、自傳

　　我在民國五十五年六月七日出生於台北的一個中產階級居住的地區。我有兩個兄弟和兩個姐妹，他們都比我小。因為我是家裡最大的孩子，當父母在別處忙於其他事情的時候，照看弟弟妹妹就一直是我的責任了。這種情形多半是常事，而非例外。

　　我的父親和母親都過著相當繁忙的生活。父親是一家貿易公司的經理，時常出去旅行，有時到台灣南部，有時到亞洲其他國家。母親是家庭主婦，但是只把一部分時間用於家務。她時常承擔一些零星工作，在我舅舅的成衣店業務忙不過來的時候，她就去幫他縫製衣服，在我伯母的小餐館人手不足的時候，她就去幫她做做飯。

　　關於我的小學時期，沒有什麼特出的可以講述的事情。我是很平常的學生，成績普普通通，只有算術例外。同愛因斯坦比起來當然差得遠了，不過我的算術一直獲得全班的最高分數。

　　在國中時期，我開始對於讀書養成濃厚的興趣。我什麼都讀：報紙、雜誌、中國小說、和西洋名著的譯本。父母因為知道我喜愛讀書，便准許我到速讀班學習三個月。我所學得的速讀技能，使得我的閱讀能力大為增加。

　　在高中時代，我的興趣自然擴展到英文書籍的閱讀。在國中時代已經對這種語文打下了基礎，現在我開始把更多的餘暇用於培養英文方面的能力。我閱讀西洋名著的簡化本，聽台北國際社區廣播

more and more of my spare time to developing my English language ability. I read simplified editions of Western classics, listened to radio plays on ICRT [4], and, of course, watched English-language movies and TV programs. My perseverance in the study of this foreign language was reflected in my grades. Upon my graduation, my parents, in order to[5] help further cultivate my language fluency, surprised me with a set of annotated English readers and cassette tapes as a present.

My English has been improving by leaps and bounds[6] and I hope to make the study of this language my major in college. At present, I have dreams of becoming a great writer and translator, but such a day —if it ever comes —is far off in the future. For the time being [7], I will continue to pursue my studies to the best of [8] my ability.

電台的廣播劇，當然也看英語的電影和電視節目。從我英文考試的成績，可以看出我對於學習這種外國語的堅持不懈的努力。在我高中畢業的時候，父母為了幫助培養我在英文寫作和口說方面的暢通，送給我一套帶注解的英文讀物和錄音帶，使我感到意外的驚喜。

我的英文進步得很快，我希望將來進大學的時候主修英文。現在我夢想自己將來成為一個大作家或翻譯家，但是那一天──如果真有那一天的話──還遙遠得很呢。在目前，我要盡最大的努力繼續學習。

注解：

(1) **look after:** attend to; be responsible for; care for; take care of.

照看；照料；照顧。

I thought the nurse was *looking after* you.

我以為護士在照看你。

He knows how to *look after* himself.

(=He knows how to protect himself and his interests.)

他知道如何照顧自己。

(2) **take on:** undertake, assume (a burden or responsibility).

承擔；承辦：擔負。

The college student *took on* a tutoring job to earn extra money.

那個大學生擔任家教賺外快。

He blamed himself for *taking on* more responsibility than he could handle.

他責備自己承擔太多責任，應付不了。

(3) **far from (being):** not at all; anything but. 遠非；一點也不。

He is *far from* (being) contented. 他毫不滿足。

(4) **ICRT:** International Community Radio Taipei.

台北社區國際廣播電台。

(5) **in order to (do something):** as a means to; to. 為了要；以便。

In order to catch the train, he hurried through his work.

為了趕火車，他急急忙忙地把工作做完。

We go to school *in order to* learn. 我們上學是為了要學東西。

注意：in order that 之後要接用名詞子句，例如：

He works hard *in order that* his family may live in comfort.

他努力工作，好讓家人過舒適的生活。

(6) **by leaps and bounds:** very rapidly. 十分迅速地；很快地。

Their business has grown *by leaps and bounds*.

他們的生意快速成長。

(7) **for the time being:** for now; for a while; temporarily. 暫時。

I don't have any letter paper, so this notebook paper will have to do *for the time being*.

我沒有信紙，只好暫時用這種筆記紙了。

(8) **to the best of:** as far as one is able to think, do, etc.

就一個人所能想到的或做到的事。

I'll do it *to the best of* my ability. 我會盡我所能去做的。

To the best of my knowledge, he is still in Hong Kong.

就我所知道的，他仍舊在香港。

評釋：

　　本文是一篇記敘文，第一、二段講述出生時地和家庭背景。第三、四、五段按照時間順序講述小學、國中和高中的求學情形。末段講述將來的志趣。

　　本文大致符合這類文章的寫作原則。做重點式的敘述，而不在枝節的事情上多費筆墨。

練 習 二 十

A.　根據本課內容，用完整的句子回答下列各問題：

1.　Where was the writer born?

2.　What responsibility did the writer have as the eldest child?

3.　What does the writer's father do?

4.　What does the writer's mother do?

5.　What was outstanding about the writer's elementary school education?

6.　In junior high school, what did the writer develop a keen interest in?

7.　How did the writer develop his English language ability in senior high school?

8.　What did the writer's parents surprise him with upon graduation?

9.　How has the writer's English been improving?

10. What does the writer have dreams of becoming?

B. 將下列各句譯成英文，儘量利用本課學過的成語：

1. 他暫時和他的表兄住在一起。

2. 我不在家的這段時間，請你幫忙照看我的花園好嗎?

3. 就我所能記得的，她的生日是今天。

4. 他擔負起照料這個孤兒（orphan）的責任。

5. 人口在很迅速地增加中。

C. 任選一題，作短文一篇：

1. My Family

2. My Future Career

19. A Typical Day in My Life

Although I lead an active life, there is still a certain routine[1] apparent in my daily activity.

My electric alarm clock goes off [2] each school day morning at 6:15. Experience has taught me to place it out of my reach[3], for in so doing I am forced to get out of bed and turn it off [4]. After stumbling across my room and silencing its buzzing noise, I grope my way[5] to the bathroom to wash up[6]. My mother is in the kitchen by this time preparing breakfast, the appetizing smell of which finds its way[7] under the bathroom door and entices me into the kitchen.

I greet my mother in the customary way and seat myself in front of a bowl of steaming congee and a dish of dried meat floss. Halfway through my breakfast I glance at my watch: as usual it reads 6:40. If I don't leave by 6:45, I'll certainly be late. I quickly finish the rest of my breakfast, grab my schoolbag, and fly out of [8] the door. No matter [9] how early I wake up, I always seem to end up [10] having to rush to the bus stop.

My classmates are usually filing into the bus as I arrive, somewhat out of breath [11].The bus stop is only a block from my house and my running to it every morning does have its good side: sprinting[12] is not only good exercise but also very invigorating first thing in the morning.

Riding on the bus, however, is very bad for one's health. A morning does not pass without[13] my being squeezed into a motorized can, without an elbow being jabbed in my ribs, and without my brightly polished shoes being stepped on and dirtied. I get off[14] the bus in front of our school, relieved to be able to move around freely in fresh open air again.

I arrive at [15] schools before 7:30, which leaves me with over half an

十九、我生活中一個典型的日子

雖然我過的是一種很繁忙的生活，在我的日常活動之中還是顯然有某種常規可循的。

在每個上課的日子，我的電鬧鐘在六點十五分就響了。根據過去經驗的教訓，我把電鬧鐘放在伸手搆不到的地方，因為這樣一來，我聽見鬧鐘的響聲不能不起床，把它關起來。我蹣跚著走過去，止住鬧鐘的警聲，然後摸索著走到浴室去洗臉。這時候，母親已經在廚房準備早餐，令人垂涎的香味從浴室門的縫隙傳過來，把我引誘到廚房去。

我以慣常的方式向母親問候，然後坐下來，前面擺著一碗熱氣騰騰的稀飯和一碟肉鬆。早餐吃了一半的時候，我匆匆地看看錶：像每天一樣，六點四十分。如果我六點四十五分不出門的話，一定要遲到的。於是我趕快吃完早飯，抓起書包，跑出門外。不論我醒得多麼早，幾乎總是必須匆匆忙忙地趕到公共汽車站。

當我有些上氣不接下氣地到達車站的時候，我的同學們通常已經在魚貫上車了。公共汽車站離我家只有一個街區，我每天早晨跑步到那裡也有好處；短距離的全速奔跑不僅是很好的運動，也是很能振奮精神的清晨第一件事。

可是，坐公共汽車卻對一個人的健康很不利。每天早晨，我總是被塞在一個摩托罐頭裡面，別人的臂肘猛撞我的肋骨，擦得很亮的皮鞋被別人踩髒。我在學校前面下車，由於可以再度在戶外的新鮮空氣之中自由走動而感到輕鬆。

我在七點三十分以前到達學校，在第一節課上課之前還有半個

hour before my first class begins; I usually spend this time glancing over[16] my lessons. The next eight hours pass in the blink of an eye[17] as I digest the knowledge instilled into my young mind.

At 4:30 the school bell dismisses us and I head[18] straight over to the athletic field for an exciting game of basketball or soccer. When it starts to get dark, I reluctantly proceed to the bus stop for my fatiguing ride home.

Our family usually eats dinner together around 7:00. My mother is an excellent cook and her hearty meals are enough to feed an army. After dinner, we all relax in the living room and enjoy some fruit while watching the evening news. Then I withdraw to the quiet of my room after the news and bury myself in[19] my schoolwork.

My eyes start to become heavy with sleep around 11:15. Before retiring[20], I wish my parents good night, brush my teeth, and set my alarm clock for another routine day.

鐘頭的時間；我總是利用這段時間把功課大略看一看，在以後的八個小時當中，我都在吸收那些被灌輸到我幼小心的心靈裡面的知識，那八個小時一轉眼就過去了。

　　四點三十分，鐘聲一響，我們都下了課了，我一直朝著運動場走去，做一些緊張刺激的遊戲，打籃球或踢足球。天黑的時候，我很不情願地前往公共汽車站，搭車回家，這又是一段使人疲勞的行程。

　　我們全家人通常在七點左右一起吃晚飯。我母親很會做菜，她總把飯食預備得很豐盛，足夠一大群人吃。晚飯後，我們都坐在起居室休息，一邊看晚間電視新聞，一邊吃一些水果。然後我就回到自己的房間，在安靜的環境之中專心做功課。

　　在十一點十五分左右，我開始有些昏昏欲睡了。在就寢之前，我向父母說晚安，刷牙，把鬧鐘撥好，以便開始另一個常規的日子。

注解：

(1) **routine:** fixed and regular way of doing things. 常規

She keeps her figure slim with a good exercise *routine*.

她以良好的運動常規保持身材的苗條。

(2) **go off:** ring, buzz, or sound loudly. 響起來。

The alarm *went off* when the robber forced open the door.

強盜闖進門時，警鈴響起來了。

(3) **out of (one's) reach:** beyond the distance that one can reach with his hands. 在伸手可以拿到的距離之外。

Put the bottle of insecticide *out of reach* of the children.

把那瓶殺蟲藥放在孩子們搆不著的地方。

注意：out of (one's) reach的相對語是within (one's) reach:

I like to have my reference books wit *with easy reach*.

(4) **turn off:** stop the flow of (water, gas, electric current, etc.)by turning a tap, pressing a switch, etc.; shut off. 關掉。

Turn off the water. 把水關掉。

Shall I *turn off* the radio? 你要把收音機關掉嗎?

注意：turn off 的相對語是 turn on.

(5) **grope one's way:** find one's way by feeling with out-stretched hands in, or as if in, the dark. 摸索著走路。

After the lights went out, he *groped his way* to the kitchen for some candles.

電燈熄了以後，他摸索著走到廚房裡去拿一些蠟燭。

(6) **wash up:** wash one's face and hands. 洗臉和手。

He *washed up* after repairing his motorcycle.

他修過機車後洗臉和手。

(7) find (one's) way: succeed in reaching. 抵達；達到。

The rescuers *found their way* to the lost campers.

救援的人們抵達了露營者的地方。

How did you *find your way* home in that fog?

霧那麼大，你是怎麼到家的?

(8) **fly out of:** rush or hurry out of. 衝出。

The students *flew out of* the classroom after class was dismissed.

學生們下課後衝出教室。

(9) **on matter:** 參看範文8，注8。

(10) **end up:** to reach or arrive at a final condition, circumstance, or goal. 結果；最後到達某種情況或目標。

If you do that, you'll *end up* in prison for sure.

你要是那樣做，最後一定會坐牢的。

He *ended up* as the head of the company.

他最後做了公司的老闆。

(11) **out of breath:** unable to take in breath quickly enough.

喘不過氣來。

(12) **sprint:** run at one's fastest speed, esp. for a short distance.
猛衝，急馳。

(13) **not... without:** no, not, never 與 without 連用，是兩個否定變成一個肯定，請參考下列各句：

You *cannot* buy things *without* money. 你沒有錢不能買東西。

They *never* meet *without* quarreling. 他們每次見面必定吵架。

Not a day passed *without* their meeting. 他們無日不見面。

(14) **get off:** leave (esp. a public vehicle). 下 (車)；下去。

I'm *getting off* (the bus) at the next stop.

我下一站就要下去（下車）了。

Where are you *getting off* the plane, sir?

先生，你在哪裡下飛機呀？

注意：get off 的相對語是 get on.

(15) **arrive at:** reach (a place, esp. the end of a journey).
到達；抵達。

We *arrived at* the station just as the train was leaving.

我們在火車快開的時候才到達車站。

注意：arrive at 通常指到達一個小地方，arrive in 指到達一個大地方。

(16) **glance over:** look at briefly or hastily. 瞥視，瞄。

He *glanced over* his speech before entering the lecture hall.

他進入演講廳之前瞄了一下他的演講詞。

(17) **in the blink of an eye:** (=in the twinkling of an eye) in an instant. 一霎眼工夫；一剎那。

The shop boy finished his errands *in the blink of an eye.*

那男店員一霎眼就辦完了差事。

(18) **head:** move in the direction indicated. 朝(某方向)前進。

(19) **bury oneself in:** become deeply involved in.

專心於；埋頭做（某件事）。

Immediately after dinner, his father *buried himself in* his paperwork.

剛吃過晚飯，他父親就埋首於文書工作。

No wonder you didn't hear me enter —you were *buried in Three's Company.*

難怪你沒有聽見我進來——原來你在專心看「三人行」。

(20) **retire:** go to bed. 就寢。

評釋 :

　　這是一個很普通的題目，應該注意的是時間和篇幅有限，不可做太詳細的敘述。本文按照順序記述起床、洗臉、吃早飯、上學、回家、做功課、就寢等事，每個項目只敘述一兩樣突出的事物。

練 習 二 十 一

A.　根據本課內容，用完整的句子回答下列各問題：

1.　How does each school day morning begin for the writer?

2.　What does he do after being forced to get out of bed?

3.　What does the writer do after greeting his mother in the customary way?

4.　What happens halfway through breakfast?

5.　What is the good side of running to the bus stop every morning?

6.　Why is riding on the bus bad for one's health?

7.　What does the writer usually do before his first class begins?

8.　Where does the writer go after school?

9.　What does the writer do after dinner?

10.　What does the writer do before retiring?

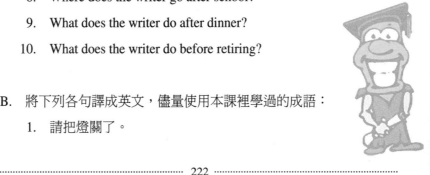

B.　將下列各句譯成英文，儘量使用本課裡學過的成語：

1.　請把燈關了。

2. 我們在台北上火車，在台中下火車。

3. 不論他躲到那裡，警察都會把他找到。

4. 他專心工作。

5. 如果你繼續每晚加班工作，歸終你會住進醫院去。

6. 他每說英語必有錯誤。

7. 在回答我的問題之前，先看看考卷（test）。

C. 任選一題，作短文一篇：

1. The Happiest (or Saddest) Day in My Life

2. My First Day of Summer Vacation

20. My First Day of Camping

The first day of our week-long camping expedition in the mountains of central Taiwan was one of learning by doing.

Wenhua and I arrived at our lake-side campsite at 11:00 on a crisp autumn morning and the scenery was spellbinding[1]. We stood by the edge of the lake drinking in [2] the changing fall colors and isolated silence. We appeared to be the only individuals for miles around[3] who were daring enough to camp out [4] at this time of year.

We were exhausted from our long trek up the steep mountain and the lake was beckoning us to[5] refresh our worn-out bodies in its soothing water. Heeding its call, we delayed setting up[6] our tent, changed into[7] our swim trunks instead, and jumped into the lake. Having been heated by the morning sun, its water was noticeably warmer than the crisp mountain air. We were enticed to play like two carefree porpoises for over an hour.

We emerged from the water with renewed vigor, and after dressing, we began to make plans for setting up camp. The tent had still to be erected and our stomachs were grumbling from hunger; the latter was given priority.

Wenhua gathered twigs and branches for the fire and I made our lunch. Our first meal was a Spartan[8] one: scrambled eggs and dried meat floss.

After lunch, I suggested we set up the tent, but Wenhua thought the preparation of firewood for our first night to be more important. Night falls early in these latitudes, he said, and the thermometer can dip to below zero. His logic was quite convincing, so I unpacked the axes and we began to chop sufficient fuel to last[9] through the night. Afterwards we

二十、露營的第一天

我們到台灣中部的山上做為期一周的露營，第一天是一個藉實際做事來學習的日子。

在一個微有寒意的秋天上午，我和文華在十一點到達湖濱露營地，那裡的景色幽美迷人。我們站在湖邊，陶醉在秋天的變化色彩和與世隔絕的寂靜之中。在周圍數里之內，我們大概是僅有的膽敢在這個時季前來露營的人。

我們走上這座陡峭的山，經過很長一段艱辛的路程才到達這個露營地，都已經精疲力竭了，現在湖似乎在向我們招手，要我們投身到那具有撫慰作用的湖水裡面，消除身體的疲憊。因此我們先不去搭帳篷，換上游泳褲，跳到湖水裡面去了。湖水已經被上午的太陽曬熱了，顯然比山中微冷的空氣更為暖和一些。我們情不自禁地像兩隻無憂無慮的海豚似的在水中玩了一個多小時。

我們從湖水裡出來，精力完全恢復了。穿好衣服之後，我們開始計劃紮營。帳篷還沒有搭起，肚子卻餓得咕嚕咕嚕地響起來了，我們決定先吃飯。

文華收集一些小樹枝和大樹枝，我做午飯。我們的第一餐是斯巴達式的：只有炒蛋和肉鬆。

午飯後，我提議把帳篷搭起來，但是文華認為把我們第一夜所需的柴薪準備起來是更為重要的。他說在這個地區，黑夜降臨很早，氣溫可以降到零下。他的道理很令人信服，於是我把斧子從背包取出，開始砍伐足夠第一夜使用的木柴。然後我們又到森林裡面尋覓一些野果和漿果。

hunted around the forest for some wild fruit and berries.

It was not long before we began to hear the buzzing of mosquitoes —a sure sign that darkness was fast approaching. And our tent still had not been unpacked. Walking back to the camp, we looked at each other thinking —what next? The answer was obvious.

This time it was Wenhua's turn to cook. He boiled some water for the instant noodles while I opened a can of fish. During dinner, we decided to rough it[10] the first night: we would sleep in the open air in our sleeping bags.

We cleaned up[11] our campsite after dinner, washed the pot, and tied our trash in a plastic bag. The cold mountain air forced us to sleep around eight o'clock.

Around midnight, a snorting sound woke me up[12]. Thinking that it was Wenhua, I gently nudged him to be quiet. But he was already awake! It was at this point that we both realized the snoring-like sounds were coming from an animal searching through our trash for a midnight snack. In our exhaustion we had forgotten to suspend our trash bag from a tall branch out of the reach[13] of nighttime scavengers, now a small bear was hungrily tearing it to shreds. Not wishing to be made into a snack ourselves, we rolled over and played dead. I thought to myself how much safer I would have felt in our tent, hidden from the wild animal's view. Fortunately the bear was contented with our trash and soon wandered off into the woods.

The next morning we surveyed the damage: scraps of paper and tin cans were scattered all about, as were our cooking utensils. We decided that we would procrastinate[14] no longer: even before cleaning up this mess, we would set up our tent.

　　不久之後。我們開始聽到蚊子的嗡嗡聲，這是黑夜即將來臨的確實徵兆。回到了營地，我們彼此互相看看，心裡在想下一步該做什麼了，答案是明顯的。

　　這次輪到文華做飯了，他燒些開水，預備泡速食麵，我則打開一罐魚。在吃晚飯的時候，我們決定第一夜過簡單而不舒適的生活：我們要用睡袋在山野中露宿。

　　晚飯後，我們把營地打掃乾淨，洗了鍋，把垃圾放在一個塑膠袋裡。山上很涼，迫使我們八點鐘左右就鑽進睡袋裡面去了。

　　午夜前後，一個噴鼻息的聲音把我吵醒了。我以為是文華打鼾，就用臂肘輕輕碰他一下，叫他安靜些。但是他已經醒了。這時候，我們兩人才知道那個類似打鼾的聲音，原來是來自一隻動物，牠正在我們的垃圾裡面尋找宵夜的食物。我們吃完飯時太疲倦了，忘記垃圾袋掛在高樹技上，使夜間覓食者搆不到，現在一隻小熊正如飢如渴地把它撕成碎片。我們不願意自己成為小熊的宵夜食品，就都轉過身去裝死。我心裡想，如果我們在帳篷裡，那隻野獸看不到，就安全得多了。幸而那些垃圾已使小熊感覺滿足，不久就走開，走到樹林裡面了。

　　第二天早晨，我們察視災情，碎紙片和空罐頭散亂在各處，廚房用具也是一樣。我們決定不能再拖延了，甚至在動手清理髒亂東西之前，就先把帳篷搭起。

注解：

(1) **spellbinding:** enchanting. 迷人的。

(2) **drink in:** absorb by eager attention. 欣賞；陶醉於…之中。

They *drank in* the dazzling fireworks display.

他們欣賞使人眼花繚亂的煙火表演。

(3) **for miles around:** 在周圍數哩之內。

There are no telephones *for miles around*.

在這周圍數哩之內都沒有電話。

(4) **camp out:** live, cook, and sleep out of doors (as in a tent).

露營。

We *camped out* on the beach all weekend.

我們整個周末都在湖濱露營。

(5) **beckon（someone）to:** make a silent sign, as with the finger, to call (someone) to. 向…招手示意；召喚。

She *beckoned* him *to* follow her.

她向他招手示意，要他跟著她。

The smell of Mother's cooking *beckoned* him *to* the kitchen.

母親烹飪的香味把他引進了廚房。

(6) **set up:** to prepare (something) for use (by assembling it).

架設；設置。

It took the TV crew several days to *set up* their equipment for the Double Ten parade.

電視台的工作人員花了幾天時間架設裝備以便轉播雙十節的閱兵。

They *set up* a stand by the roadside an sold fruit.

他們在路邊擺了一個攤子賣水果。

(7) **change into:** 換上（某種衣服）。

He *changed into* something more comfortable after returning home from the office.

他下班回家後換上舒適的衣服。

The bride *changed into* a *ch'i pao* after the wedding ceremony.

婚禮完畢後新娘子換上一件旗袍。

(8) **Spartan:** suggestive of the ancient Spartans; sternly disciplined and rigorously simple, frugal, or austere.

斯巴達式的；簡單的。

(9) **last:** be enough; go on. 足夠；維持；持續。

We have enough food to *last* three days.

我們現有的食物足以維持三天。

(10) **rough it:** 參看範文8，注7。

(11) **clean up:** make clean or tidy; put in order; clean everything.

收拾乾淨；清理。

You should always *clean up* after a picnic.

野餐過後你應該收拾乾淨。

We should *clean up* the place before the guests arrive.

在客人來到之前我們應該把這地方清理一下。

It's your turn to *clean* the dormitory room *up*.

現在輪到你打掃宿舍的房間了。

(12) **wake up:** rouse from sleep; become conscious after a sleep.

醒來；喚醒；吵醒。

I *wake up* every morning at seven o'clock.

我每天早晨七點鐘醒來。

Don't make so much noise —you'll *wake* the baby *up*.

不要弄出這麼大的聲音來，你會吵醒孩子的。

(13) **out of (one's) reach:** 參看範文 20，注 3。

(14) **procrastinate:** delay (repeatedly and without good reason) in doing some necessary act. 耽擱；拖延。

He *procrastinated* until it was too late.

他拖延很久，以致太晚了。

John *procrastinate*d from week to week about giving up smoking.

約翰一個禮拜又一個禮拜地拖延戒煙。

評釋：

　　本文是一篇敘述文。按照時間順序敘述露營第一天所發生的事情：到達、游泳、午飯、採集柴薪和野果、晚飯、就寢。

　　本文有一個基本的主題，就是搭帳篷。作者曾多次提到未能搭帳篷。到倒數第二段出現高潮。由於未搭帳篷而有驚險的遭遇。

練　習　二　十　二

A. 根據本課內容，用完整的句子回答下列各問題：

　1. What kind of day was the first day of their week-long camping expedition?

　2. When did they arrive at their lake-side campsite?

　3. What did they do by the edge of the lake?

　4. Why did they delay setting up their tent?

　5. What did they do after emerging from the lake?

　6. What did they do after lunch?

　7. How did they know darkness was fast approaching?

　8. What did they decide during dinner?

　9. What did they do after dinner?

　10. What happened around midnight?

　11. What did they do the next morning?

B. 將下列各句譯成英文，儘量使用本課學過的成語：

1. 她為了舉行茶會而把房子打掃乾淨。

2. 他換上了工作服。

3. 我們露營一星期。

4. 他們在路邊擺攤（stand）賣水果。

5. 請在五點鐘叫醒我。

C. 任選一題，作短文一篇：

1. A Rainy Day

2. Leisure Time

21. The Most Pleasant Surprise in My Life

I had always wanted to meet a film star, especially one of the great martial arts actors of the Bruce Lee type.

We had participated in a China Youth Corps activity at the beach that summer. At its conclusion, several of us decided to stay on[1] a few more days and enjoy some of the things which were impractical to do in a large group.

Two friends and I had decided to take a trip in a motorboat to an island a short distance away. We got up quite early and, having gone without[2] breakfast, we arrived at the boat landing by half past eight. We had to wait there until nine, however, because the boatman was late. We passed the time building sandcastles and digging for sand crabs.

After the boatman arrived, we released the half dozen sand crabs we had caught and boarded his vessel. It promised to be a fine day, and we were glad that we had dressed in light T-shirts and jeans. The boatman was quite friendly and seemed in on hurry, for business was slack at that hour.

As we neared the island we suddenly saw a beautiful yacht anchored in a hidden cove. The boatman asked us whether we would like to have a closer look, to which we readily replied "Yes." As we approached, a bearded foreigner appeared and called out, "Like to come aboard?" This was a wonderful opportunity to see a yacht, so we eagerly walked up the steps of the gangway. Imagine our delight when the bearded stranger invited us to spend the day on the yacht! Without hesitation, we agreed and asked the boatman to return for us at five o'clock that afternoon.

Our delight turned into rapture when we learned in whose company

二十一、我生平最愉快的意外遭遇

我一直想遇見一位電影明星，尤其是像李小龍那一型的武功高超的演員。

那年夏天，我們去參加救國團在海濱舉辦的一項活動。在活動結束的時候，我們之中有幾個人決定在那裡多留幾天，去欣賞一些一個大團體不方便去欣賞的景物。

我和兩個朋友決定乘汽艇到一個距離不遠的島上一遊。我們那天起得很早，沒吃早飯，八點半就到達汽艇碼頭了。可是，我們必須在那裡等到九點鐘，因為船夫遲到。我們在海灘上建築沙堡，並且挖掘沙蟹。

船夫來了，我們把捉到的六隻沙蟹都放走了，上了他的船。天氣看起來會是晴朗的，因此我們對於自己只穿了很薄的運動衫和牛仔褲，覺得很高興。船夫十分和氣，似乎也不急著趕路，因為那個時候生意很清淡。

我們駛近那個島嶼的時候，忽然看見一隻漂亮的遊艇停泊在一個隱秘的小灣裡。船夫問我們願意不願意到近處看一看，我們欣然回答說：「願意.」當我們駛近遊艇的時候，一個留鬍子的外國人出現了，高聲喊道：「願意上來玩玩嗎？」這將是一個參觀遊艇的大好機會，於是我們很熱切地沿著舷梯走上去。那個留鬍子的陌生人邀請我們在遊艇上玩一天，你可以想像得出我們是如何地高興。我們毫不猶豫地同意的，請船夫下午五點再來接我們。

當我們曉得我們是和什麼人在一起的時候，我們的高興轉為狂

we were. It was Jackie Chan[3] and Chuck Norris[4], the two world-famous kung fu actors. They were on location[5] filming scenes for their upcoming[6] American-made movie. Many big stars try to avoid their fans, especially the young ones, but Jackie and Chuck were quite sociable and treated us like old friends. After showing us around[7] the yacht, they invited us to watch how a kung fu movie was made.

We followed them a short way inland to the place where they were shooting. We stood spellbound[8] as they practiced their fight scene —two champion[9] fighters pitted one against[10] the other. They didn't appear to be playacting[11], for they were exchanging real blow for real blow.

After a delicious lunch, we sunbathed on the deck of the yacht, listening to Jackie and Chuck reminisce about[12] their acting experiences. They even showed us how they "pulled their punches" [13] so as not to hurt each other. All too quickly, five o'clock arrived and we thanked everyone for their hospitality.

Yes, this adventure was surely the most pleasant surprise in my young life.

喜了。在我們面前的原來是馳名國際的功夫演員成龍和諾禮斯。他們是在那裡為一部即將推出的美國影片拍攝外景。許多大明星都避免和他們的影迷接觸，尤其是年輕的影迷。但是諾禮斯和成龍的態度很友善，把我們當作老朋友一般看待，他們先領我們到遊艇各處參觀一番，然後便請我們去看一部功夫片是如何拍成的。

我們跟隨他們往內陸走了很短的一段路，到達他們拍攝電影的場所。他們練習打鬥的場面。兩位第一流打鬥者互相對抗，那個景象使我們站在那裡如醉如癡，完全被迷住了。他們不像是在演戲，因為他們真在對打！

在吃過一頓美味的午餐之後，我們躺在遊艇甲板上做日光浴，聽成龍和諾禮斯講述他們演電影的經驗。他們甚至於表演給我們看他們如何「在打鬥時故意不使出全力」，以免互相傷害。時間過得太快了，不覺已到了五點鐘，我們為了所受的慇懃款待而向艇上所有的人們道謝。

這次奇遇的確是我有生以來最愉快的意外遭遇。

注解:

(1) **stay on:** remain after the usual or expected time of leaving.

在通常預期應該離去的時候仍然留在某處。

Dr. Li will be 65 next month, but he will *stay on* as chairman.

李博士下個月就滿六十五歲了,但他要繼續留下當主任。

(2) **go without:** be, manage, or get along without; lack.

沒有;缺乏。

He *went without* food for three days. 他三日未食。

A poor man has to *go without* many things, which a rich man regards as necessities of life.

有很多富人認為是生活必需品的東西,窮人根本享受不到。

(3) **Jackie Chan:** Chinese kung fu actor. 成龍(中國功夫演員)。

(4) **Chuck Norris:** 諾禮斯(美國武打電影明星)。

(5) **on location:** in or at a particular place (outside the studio) for filming a particular movie, scene, etc. 拍攝外景。

(6) **upcoming:** about to take place, appear, or be presented.

即將舉行的;即將來臨的;即將上演的。

(7) **show around:** serve as a guide; conduct on a visit or a tour.

引導各處參觀;導遊。

My cousin is visiting us next week, and I've promised to *show* him *around* Taipei.

我表弟下星期要來看我們,我答應帶他遊台北。

(8) **spellbound:** enchanted or fascinated.著迷的。

(9) **champion:** first-rate. 第一流的；最好的。

(10) **pit against**: match against; put in opposition to; place in competition or rivalry with.

使…與…對抗；以…與…對抗。

The little man *pitted* his brains *against* the big man's strength.

那個小個兒用他的智力對抗那個大個兒的力氣。

He couldn't find someone to *pit* his skill and courage *against*.

他找不到一個人能對抗他的技巧和勇氣。

(11) **playact:** pretend; behave with an unreal show of feeling, etc.

假裝；演戲。

She's not really crying —she's just *playacting* so that you'll feel sorry for her.

她並不是真的在哭——她是假裝的，好讓你為她難過。

(12) **reminisce about:** talk or think about (the past).

回憶或追懷（往事）。

They stayed up half the night *reminiscing about* their high school days. 他們待到半夜，追懷他們的中學時代。

(13) **pull (one's) punches:** not to hit as hard as one really can.

（拳擊時）故意不用力；未使出全力。

應用進階篇

評釋：

　　本文除首段為引言、末段為結語外，按照時間的順序敘述自己的一項意外遭遇。本文的特點是以輕鬆的筆調平鋪直敘，顯得自然而親切，所以段落比較多。

練 習 二 十 三

A. 根據本課內容，用完整的句子回答下列各問題：

1. Who had the writer always wanted to meet?

2. Why did the narrator and several of his friends decide to stay on a few more days?

3. What had the writer and his two friends decided to do?

4. How did they pass the time while waiting for the boat to arrive?

5. How were they dressed?

6. What did they see as they neared the island?

7. What happened as they approached the yacht?

8. When did their delight turn into rapture?

9. What were the two world-famous kung fu stars doing there?

10. Why didn't the two champion fighters appear to be playacting?

11. What did the writer and his friends do after lunch?

B. 將下列各句譯成英文，儘量利用本課學過的成語：

1. 他沒吃晚飯，可是他還繼續工作。

2. 他用自己的耐力和另一個人的速度對抗。

3. 經理領我們參觀工廠。

4. 管家同意留下，直到找到代替的人（replacement）的時候為止。

5. 我最要好的朋友和我在一起談我們童年的事情。

C. 任選一題，作短文一篇：

1. A Lucky (or Unlucky) Experience

2. Daydreaming.

IV. 議論文 (Argumentative Essays)

22. Is Television Harmful to Children?

The potential effects of television on children are both positive and negative; unfortunately, in present-day society, the negative effects outweigh[1] the positive.

On the positive side, television is a vast encyclopedia of knowledge. A special[2] on European politics follows a Chinese historical drama, mountain climbing in the Himalayas comes before a study of threatened wildlife, and Peking opera gives way to[3] Chinese culture shorts [4]. A child can absorb —and retain —more information from an hour of watching educational programs in his living room than he can from a day in a stuffy library.

Television can also serve to stimulate the fertile imagination of the young. Quiz shows can not only increase a child's store of knowledge on a variety of subjects, but also stimulate him to learn more about such subjects on his own[5]. Sports competitions —both local and international —offer children glimpses of [6] top athletic skills worthy of imitation.

In spite of [7] these benefits, the negative influences of television have been extremely harmful to the young. Children are very naive and do not have enough experience to realize that TV shows present an unreal world, that commercials purposely mislead TV viewers in order to[8] sell products that are sometimes bad or useless. Children believe and want to imitate what they see. This is especially true when children watch animated cartoons, where violence is the most frequent method used by "the good guys" to overcome "the bad." Most psychologists agree that the "television generations" are far more violent than their parents or grandparents.

二十二、電視對兒童有害嗎？

電視對於兒童可能發生的影響，有正反兩個方面；不幸在目前的社會裡，壞的影響超過了好的影響。

就好的方面來說，電視可以說是一部浩大的知識百科全書。一個有關歐洲政治的特別節目，隨著一部中國歷史劇出現；在攀登喜馬拉雅山的影片之後，播映一篇有關野生動物遭受威脅的研究；平劇為一些中國文化短片所接替。兒童在起居室看一小時教育性節目所吸收——並且記住——的知識，多於在空氣不流通的圖書館裡讀一整天書的收穫。

電視也可以刺激孩子們的豐富想像力。猜謎節目不僅能使孩子增長許多方面的知識，也可以激使他自己設法就這些方面知道更多的東西。運動比賽——本地的和國際性的——使兒童看到一些值得模仿的最優秀的運動技能。

儘管電視有這些好處，它的不良影響對於兒童也是極其有害的。兒童很天真，沒有足夠的生活經驗，因而不曉得電視表演所呈現的是一個虛幻的世界，商業廣告為了推銷一些有時是很不好或無用的產品，故意欺騙電視觀眾。兒童們往往相信他們所看到的東西，並且想要模仿。他們在看卡通片的時候，尤其如此，在那些卡通片裡，暴力是「好人」制服「壞人」所最常使用的手段。大多數心理學家都認為「電視時代的人們」比他們的父母那一輩或祖父母那一輩更為兇暴得多。

Some people argue that the living room is surely a more healthy place of entertainment than a dark and smoky movie theater. This, however, is a matter for the parent. Far too many parents do not exercise their authority over[9] what programs their children view. Instead, television is used as a nursemaid or as a babysitter for a restless or cranky child; and more often than not, it is the violent cartoons or morally questionable soap operas[10] that produce the calming effect.

Other people argue that fast-paced TV programs make young people more quick-witted and alert. On the surface, this argument appears to have its merits; but upon closer examination, this apparent benefit is more like "a wolf in sheep's clothing." [11] For the truth of the matter is that action-packed[12] programs have made the young less patient. They have become so accustomed to[13] TV shows, where everything is quick and entertaining, that they do not have the patience to read an article lacking color illustrations, to read a book which requires thought, or to listen to a teacher who doesn't do funny things like the people do on children's programs. And they expect all problems to be solved happily in ten, fifteen, or thirty minutes, for that's the time it takes on the screen.

It is certain that television has had a profound influence on children. It is also certain that, along with its benefits, it has brought enormous problems. To these problems we must soon find a solution because, whether we like it or not, television is here to stay.

　　有些人主張，起居室確然是一個比昏暗而煙霧瀰漫的電影院更為有益健康的消遣之所。可是，這件事情就要看做父母的人如何處理了。太多的父母對於子女所看的電視節目並沒有行使他們的權力。對於一個不安靜的或暴躁的孩子，做父母的反而利用電視，當做照看小孩的女僕或隨臨時受顧照看小孩的人；能對兒童發生安撫作用的，往往是那些宣揚暴力的卡通片或在道德方面有問題的連續劇。

　　有些人認為，快步調的電視節目可以把兒童訓練得更為才思敏捷而機警。從表面看起來，這種論調也有它的道理，但是經過更仔細的檢討之後，這種表面上的利益卻更像是一隻「蒙著羊皮的狼」。因為實際的情形是，那些充滿緊張和暴力場面的節目已經使兒童們更沒有耐性。他們已經完全習慣於一切都很快速而有趣味的電視節目，因而沒有耐心去讀一篇沒有彩色插圖的文章，去看一本需要思考的書，去聆聽一位不能像兒童節目裡面的人們那樣做出可笑行為的教師講課。他們預期一切問題都可以在十分鐘、十五分鐘、或三十分鐘內圓滿解決，因為那是在螢光幕上解決問題所需要的時間。

　　電視已經對於兒童發生深遠的影響，這是不容置疑的事。在電視的各種好處之外，它已經帶來了一些巨大的問題，這也是不容置疑的事。對於那些問題，我們必須早些想出一個解決辦法，因為不管你喜歡也罷，不喜歡也罷，電視是要長久存在下去的。

注解：

(1) **outweigh:** be greater in weight, value, or importance than.
勝過；超過。

My love for her *outweighs* everything else.
我對她的愛勝過其他一切。

(2) **special:** single televised program not part of a regular series.
特別節目。

(3) **give way to:** become less useful or important. 為…所取代。
Steam trains *gave way to* electric trains.
蒸汽火車為電動火車所取代。

(4) **short:** a short, often documentary or educational, program of film. 短片；短的節目。

(5) **on one's own:** by oneself; without help. 獨自；自力。
To start life *on one's own* requires much self-sacrifice but the rewards may be great.
自力開創人生需要很大的犧牲，但可能獲得很多的益處。

(6) **offer (one) a glimpse of:** enable (one) to have a vague idea about. 使看到。
Science fiction movies *offer* us *a glimpse of* the future.
科幻電影使我們看到未來。
The tour *offered* us *a glimpse of* American culture.
這次旅行使我們看到了美國的文化。

(7) **in spite of:** despite; not withstanding; in disregard or defiance of. 儘管⋯仍然。

I will go *in spite of* the storm.

我要冒著暴風雨前往。

In spite of all my urgings, he continues to smoke.

儘管我勸了又勸，他還是繼續抽煙。

(8) **in order to (do something):** 參看範文18，注5。

(9) **exercise... over:** use (influence, authority, power, etc.) in dealing with somebody. 對⋯行使(影響力，權力等)。

He *exercised* his influence *over* the manager to get me the job.

他利用他對經理的影響力替我找到這個工作。

Hitler *exercised* some strange power *over* the German people.

希特勒對德國人民行使奇特的權力。

(10) **soap opera:** a radio or television serial drama of a highly melodramatic, sentimental nature (so called because many such programs were sponsored by soap companies).（廣播或電視之）連續劇（因多由肥皂粉公司提供者，故名）。

(11) **a wolf in sheep's clothing:** a person who has evil intentions but who appears to be harmless. 面善心惡的人。

(12) **action-packed:** full of exciting scenes, esp. violent ones. 充滿緊張場面的；（尤指）充滿暴力場面的。

(13) **accustomed to:** 參看範文5，注1。

評釋：

　　這是一篇議論文。

　　作者在第一段就明明白白地說出他的意見；電視對學童的影響有好的方面，也有壞的方面。

　　第二、三段說明電視節目對兒童的好處。

　　第四、五、六段說明電視節目對兒童所產生的不良影響。

　　最末一段和第一段相呼應。結論是應該針對電視節目的缺點加以改進。

　　應該注意的是，在作議論文的時候，必須舉出正確的理由，來支持自己的觀點，才能站得住腳。

練 習 二 十 四

A.　根據本課內容，用完整的句子回答下列各問題：

1.　What is one of the positive effects of television on children?

2.　What is the other positive effect of television on children?

3.　How is television used by many parents?

4.　Why are fast-paced TV programs more like a "wolf in sheep's clothing"?

5.　What profound influence has television had on children?

B. 將下列各句譯成英文，儘量使用本課學過的成語：

1. 他辛勤工作，為的是使他的家人生活舒適。(用in order to)

2. 儘管遭遇種種困難，我們還是成功了。

3. 我已經習慣於這種工作。

4. 為了使每個學生都能懂，教師把那一段一再地講解。 (用in order that)

5. 你能獨自做這項工作嗎?

6. 中國父母對於子女運用很大的權威。

C. 任選一題，作短文一篇：

1. Should Electronic Games Be Banned?

2. Is Obtaining a College Degree Necessary?

23. Do You Believe That "The Best Things in Life Are Free"?

I agree only partly with[1] the common saying that the best things in life are free. Although it is true that Nature[2] provides us with much that is pleasant in life, there are some things which are enjoyable because of the effort required to achieve them.

Certainly Nature provides us with much free entertainment and enjoyment. There is nothing more exhilarating than[3] a beautiful sunset with colorful clouds drifting across the sky, or than some awe-inspiring form such as a lofty mountain or a stormy sea. The natural elements in their varying forms —whether they be calm and beautiful sunny days of tress being bent by gusty winds —give us a kind of free entertainment which nothing can surpass. Landscapes, whether peaceful or majestic, lakes, rivers, and twinkling stars —all fall into[4] this category.

One of the best things in life is undeniably free: friendship. Knowing we can rely on[5] a certain friend during our time of need is one of the finest feelings a human being can have. And, to be sure[6], friendship is a two-way street, for there is also a great pleasure in being able to give of ourselves[7] freely and without thought of personal gain.

Enjoyment of artistic things is also free. We need not buy a single picture to be able to view to our heart's content[8] some beautiful building or statue. We need not be experts to fully enjoy an exhibition in the local museum, which in essence[9] is a free exhibition; and we have only to visit a temple or a memorial to appreciate examples of stunning architecture.

Yet many of us, the women in particular[10], will say that the wearing of fine clothes gives a thrill[11] which is rarely surpassed. To be able to wear

二十三、你相信「世間最美好的東西都是免費的」嗎?

「世間最美好的東西都是免費的,」對於這句俗話,我只同意一部分。我們生活當中固然有許多使人愉悅的東西是由造物主提供的,可是也有一些能為我們帶來樂趣的東西,需要我們經過一番努力才能取得。

的確,造物主供給我們免費的愉悅和歡樂。最使人看了高興的,莫過於由滿天雲霞陪襯著的夕陽,和諸如高山或波濤洶湧的海洋之類使人產生敬畏之感的形狀。以各種不同形式表現出來的自然的力量,不論是平靜而美麗的晴朗日子,還是被強風颳得彎曲的樹木,都給與我們一種為任何其他東西所不能勝過的免費愉悅。平靜的或莊嚴的風景、湖泊、河流和閃耀的星辰,都屬於這一類。

人生當中有一種最美好的東西,無可否認地是免費的,那就是友情。知道自己在患難的時候有某一個朋友可以仰仗,這是人類的最美好的感受之一。的確,友誼是一條雙行道,因為如果能夠很豪爽地奉獻自己的力量去幫助別人,完全不為個人的利益著想,也會給我們帶來很大的快樂。

對於藝術的欣賞也是免費的。我們不必買一幅圖畫,就能飽覽一座美麗的建築物或雕像。我們不必身為專家,就能充分欣賞本地博物館的一項展覽,那項展覽也等於是免費的;我們只須去參觀一所廟宇或紀念館,就能鑒賞到一些極為出色的建設的實例。

可是許多人 —— 特別是女人 —— 會說,穿漂亮衣服能給與我們一種很少能為其他感受所超過的快感。能夠在所有場合都穿著第一

for every occasion the clothing of some top fashion store is the dream of many, but it requires a large bank balance[12]. A fine car to get around[13] in is also desirable, but we must first have a high-paying job to be able to afford gas and maintenance.

One of the finest things we can ever enjoy, which may be free or may be costly —not only in terms of[14] money but in energy and resolution —is the achievement of our ambitions. One's goal in life may be to become a top surgeon or engineer, a renowned fashion designer, or a successful businessman; but no matter[15] what one's choice is, only the individual person knows whether his achievements are costly or free.

Perhaps the least costly and most rewarding attainment is that of spiritual peace. How many people reach this height without superhuman effort is difficult to say, but certainly in terms of money it is free.

Thus we may say that on the whole[16] some of the best things in life are free, but there are many for which we must pay a high price.

流時裝店製作的衣服，是許多人的夢想，但是這要在銀行有大筆存款。乘一部漂亮汽車各處走動，也是令人想望的事，但是我們必須先有高薪的職業，才能付得起汽油錢和保養費。

還有一種我們所能享受到的最美好的事情，就是我們的雄心壯志的達成，這件事可以是免費的，也可以是很昂貴的，不僅從金錢方面來說，也要從體力和決心方面來說。一個人的人生目標也許是作一個第一流外科醫生或工程師，或著名的時裝設計家，或成功的商人；但是不論他所選擇的目標是什麼，只有他自己知道他的成就究竟是代價昂貴的，還是免費的。

最不昂貴而最有益的成就，也許是心靈的平靜。有多少人不經過一番超人的努力而能達到這個高的境界，是很難說的，但是從金錢的觀點來說，這種成就一定是免費的。

因此，大體而言，我們可以說，人生當中有些最美好的東西是免費的，但是有許多美好的事物，我們必須付出很高的代價，才能得到。

注解：

(1) **agree with:** agree with 後面接用某人，指你和他的意見相同，例如：

I quite *agree with* you on that point.

關於那一點，我十分同意你的看法。

I *agree with* neither side. 我任何一方都不同意。

agree to 後面接用一項意見、建議、條件、陳述、事情等，其義為「同意」、「答應」、或「接受」，通常具有一種含義；在同意之後還要執行，例如：

I find it impossible to *agree to* your terms.

我覺得要同意你的條件是不可能的事。

Mary's father has *agreed to* her marrying john.

瑪莉的父親已經答應她跟約翰結婚。

agree with後面也可以接用一項意見、建議、陳述等，意思是「同意」或「贊成」，常無執行的含義，例如：

I *agree with* all you say。你所說的我全部贊成。

I don't *agree with* buying children expensive presents.

我不贊成買貴重的禮物給小孩子。

I *agree with* his plan to hire a watchman.

我贊成他雇一個看守人的計劃。

(2) **Nature:** the force that controls the phenomena of the physical world.

大自然；造物主。

(3) **there's nothing more (adj.) than... :**...is the most (adj.)

最⋯的莫過於。

There's nothing more thoughtful *than* an unexpected gift.

最能表示關切的東西莫過於一件意外的禮物。

There's nothing that would make me *happier than* to pass the Joint College Extrance Exam.

最使我感到快樂的事莫過於通過大學聯考。

(4) **fall into:** have a definite position in a classification or an arrangement; be a part of (some category, topic, etc.)

屬於；歸入。

This phrase *falls into* a special class of idiom.

這個片語屬於一類特殊的成語。

The strange insect does not *fall into* any known class.

這種奇怪的昆蟲不屬於已經知道的任何一類。

(5) **rely on:** trust; depend on. 信賴；依賴。

You may *rely on* me to help you. 你可以信賴我幫助你。

Can we *rely on* you to be there? 我們能信賴你去那裡嗎?

One can't always *rely on* the weather. 天氣是常常靠不住的。

(6)　**to be sure:** without a doubt; certainly; surely. 的確；當然

To be sure, some people may disagree, but that doesn't mean you are wrong.

的確，有些人可能會不同意，但那並不是說你是錯的。

(7)　**give of oneself:** give one's time and effort (to help others).

奉獻自己的時間和力量 (去幫助旁人)。

You should *give* more *of* yourself by helping out at the orphanage.

你應該多奉獻自己，去孤兒院幫忙。

(8)　**to one's heart's content:** as much as one wants; to the extent that brings satisfaction. 盡情。

The children played in the park *to their heart's content*.

小孩子們在公園裡盡情地玩。

The guests danced *to their heart's content*. 客人盡情地跳舞.

(9)　**in essence:** essentially; basically; practically speaking.

在本質上；實際上。

Although he says he is a businessman, *in essence* he is really a politician.

雖然他說他是商人，實際上他是位政治人物。

Preventing pollution is not a question of technology; *in essence* it is a question of money.

防止污染並不是技術問題；在本質上，是錢的問題。

(10)　**in particular:** 參看範文14，注 2。

(11) **thrill:** sudden very strong feeling of joy, excitement, pleasure, fear, etc. that seems to flow round the body like a wave.

快樂透頂；緊張刺激；毛骨悚然。

I got a *thrill* out of running into him in the U.S.

我在美國遇到他真是高興極了。

(12) **bank balance:** （存款人在銀行的）存款（尤指支取後之餘額）。

(13) **get around:** move about; go to different places. 各處走動。

Jack's father really *gets around*: Monday he was in Tokyo; Wednesday he was in Hong Kong; and today he is in Singapore.

傑克的父親行蹤飄忽：他星期一在東京，星期三在香港，今天在新加坡。

(14) **in terms of:** 參見範文13，注 5。

(15) **no matter:** 參見範文8，注8。

(16) **on the whole:** in general. 大體上說，一般說來。

On the whole, the economy is improving.

大體上說，經濟已經好轉。

評釋：

這也是一篇議論文。

作者在第一段說明他的意見。「世間最美好的東西是免費的」，對於這句俗話，他只部分同意。

第二段說明大自然提供的許多美景，都是免費的。

第三段說明友誼是不須花錢的。

第四段說明藝術和音樂事物的欣賞，也不需要花什麼錢。

第五段說明穿好衣服坐好汽車等物質享受，必須有錢。

第六段說明自己志願的實現，也許不須花錢，也許要付出昂貴的代價。

第七段說獲得心靈的寧靜不須花錢。

末段做出結論，重申首段提出的意見。

練 習 二 十 五

A. 根據本課內容，用完整的句子回答下列各問題：

1. What does the writer only partly agree with?

2. What free entertainment and enjoyment does Nature provide us with?

3. What is one of the best things in life that is undeniably free?

4. What enjoyment is also free?

5. What does it require to be able to wear for every occasion the clothing of some top fashion store?

6. What must we have first if we want a fine car to get around in?

7. What is one of the finest things we can ever enjoy?

8. What is the least costly and most rewarding attainment?

B. 將下列各句譯成英文，儘量使用本課學過的成語：

1. 你在城裡各處走動都使用什麼交通工具? 坐公共汽車嗎?

2. 他同意了付款的條件。

3. 我同意你的意見。

4. 他是不可信賴的。

5. 他盡情大吃一頓，後來胃痛（stomachache）。

6. 不論他說什麼，對我都是一樣。

7. 感冒的時候，最好的辦法莫過於休息。

C. 任選一題，作短文一篇：

1. Should School Uniforms Be Abolished?

2. Do You Believe That "Birds of a Feather Flock Together"?

習題解答

　　本書的翻譯練習可以有不同的做法，而結果同樣正確。所以在翻譯方面所提供的答案，僅供參考之用。

練 習 一

I

A. Detailed　　B. Narrative　　C. Direct　　D. Descriptive

II

A. Suggestive　　　　　B. Narrative

C. Comparison or contrast　　D. Prediction

III

My friends……

That evening……

Here is……

練 習 二

A. 使各段互相啣接的字或片語：

not yet, after a few weeks, sound is fun, special sounds

B. 各段中使各句互相啣接的字或片語：

    a. 第一段：so far as she is concerned, the helpless tot, certainly

    b. 第二段：apparently, they, later, at first, but... it, yes

    c. 第三段：all these, one day, she laughs, now

練 習 三

A. 1. Some characteristics of the writer's neighbors are their capacity for borrowing, their capacity for creating noise, their attempt to keep up with the Huangs their readiness to give opinions, and their pets.

    2. They borrow a bottle of milk, a box of cube sugar, the writer's bicycle and toys.

    3. It does not matter what day it is or what time of day, they just love to make noise by giving noisy living room concerts or turning up their stereo system.

4. The Changs painted their gate in exactly the same color as that of the Huangs' gate, and they bought the same television set, the same washing machine, and the same car as the Huangs did.

5. The opinions the Changs give to the Huangs are in reference to some shortcoming of the Huangs.

6. Because the Changs' pets have free access to the Huangs' backyard garden.

7. Because when the Changs went traveling during summer vacation last year, the writer felt lonely for the whole time.

B. 1. I have told you everything I know in reference to the affair.

2. We went to see Mr. Chang, who gave us a hearty welcome.

3. He had no sooner arrived than he fell sick.

4. I saved him from death.

5. He cannot keep up with the class.

6. This book is superior to the other in style.

7. I got up early so that I might be in time for the first train.

8. She is fond of reading.

9. These goods are inferior to the sample.

10. I am tired of eating boiled eggs every morning.

11. He is no longer a young man.

練 習 四

A. 1. A bowl of soybean milk and a piece of bread and jam were hastily arranged for breakfast.

2. Everyone is too excited to eat breakfast, for the moving van has just pulled up outside.

3. His mother is very busy stuffing packing paper into bowls and cups, while his father is banging nails into a wooden case full of books and magazines.

4. They enter the house, full of hearty, good humor. They display an obvious willingness to lighten the writer's family's burden by taking full responsibility for the move.

5. The writer makes sure that his 'ten-speed' is safely packed and his younger brother sees that his baseball equipment is not forgotten.

6. Because to them such a sight is a form of free entertainment in their rather uneventful lives.

7. The writer's father makes a last, careful inspection of the premises, looking into every corner and cupboard.

8. He lingers in the living room for a nostalgic minute.

9. He gives a shrug, and whistles for the dog before he joins the rest of his family in the taxi.

B. 1. Please lend me a hand to move the bookshelf.

2. The bottle is full of ink.

3. I will look into the matter.

4. Where did the accident take place?

5. I can't help thinking that you are a wicked man.

6. I will see that everything is properly arranged.

7. The bed is too short for me to sleep in.

8. At last he has finished his homework.

9. In any case, I will try to come.

10. Don't leave your umbrella behind.

11. I think there is a train at 6:30, but you'd better make sure.

12. Turn the gas off when you finish cooking dinner.

練 習 五

A. 1. The chief pleasure of city life lies in its lively tempo, which stimulates every cell in one's body.

2. The noise of traffic, of people coming and going in large numbers, is nourishment to the city dweller.

3. If a spare part is wanted, there is never a long delay, for stocks are well supplied; if the latest disco record is desired, it can be purchased at any of hundreds of record stores; if a change in cuisine is longed for, there are restaurants specializing in food from almost every province in China to

choose from.

4. Without purchasing a single article, a morning's enjoyment may be had from simply looking at the latest goods displayed in the most temping manner.

5. For entertainment in the big city, one can go to first-run theaters, amusement centers, variety halls, bowling alleys, and skating rinds.

6. If Mother wants a plumber, or Father an electrician, a call on the telephone will bring one in an instant. If Mary wants the cosmetics she saw advertised on television one evening, it is a certainty that she will be able to buy them the next day. If little Johnny needs a mechanic for his bicycle, he need only go to a short distance before finding a repair shop.

7. The greatest pleasure of living in a big city is the happy feeling of being in the know.

B. 1. The money is at our disposal.

2. I am at a loss what to say. （或 I am at a loss for words.）

3. He gained wealth at the cost of this honor.

4. I long for an opportunity of seeing you.

5. He is always readily available when you need him.

6. I have to leave early.

7. His illness added to the family's trouble.

8. Her attractiveness lies in her eyes.

練 習 六

A. 1. In the handicraft department of a large department store, one can find glazed ceramic vases, porcelain tea sets, green jade figurines, imitation Ch'ing snuff bottles, and others.

2. Stylish dinnerware—white dishes with modest pale-blue edging, and intricately carved ivory chopsticks—can be found in the housewares department.

3. We can find sporting goods, camera equipment, pendant lamps, pens, stationery, watches, pocket calculators, radios, tape recorders, microwave ovens, and television sets.

4. The atmosphere is not experienced elsewhere because everyone is so busy coming and going, untiring escalators silently move their way up and down, elevators load and unload, sales personnel dart here and there, and customer bumps customer on the wide stairs.

5. The prospective buyer doesn't have to hurry because he need not buy anything at all.

6. In the department store, besides shopping, one can play electronic games, sip Colombian coffee in a cozy coffee shop, enjoy frangrant tea and tasty snacks at a Cantonese

restaurant, have a full-course meal in one of the several restaurants, or enjoy a first-run movie in one of the plush theaters.

7. To many of us no place is more fascinating than a large department store.

B. 1. When a friend gave him a ticket to the basketball game. he could not help but go.

2. This chapter adds to the value of the book.

3. We couldn't help but go to the dinner party.

4. I enjoyed the novel so much that I lost all track of time.

5. On the whole, I thought it was a fair decision.

練 習 七

A. 1. It is said that the children of the natives on Orchid Island and some South Sea islands can often swim before they can walk.

2. Learning to swim is especially important in modern times because there is so much travel than formerly.

3. When an airplane is forced to come down in the ocean, those who can swim have a better chance of surviving than those who can't.

4. Many people have avoided drowning in a boating accident because they know how to swim to shore or float in the water and wait for someone to rescue them.

5. Skill in swimming may not only result in the saving of one's own life, but in the rescuing of others who are in danger of drowning.

6. One must have confidence, and not be afraid of letting his head go under the water occasionally.

7. Learning to swim is worth while because it may enable us to save a life—maybe even our own.

B. 1. It isn't worthwhile going there.

2. The work of the office will be easy when you get accustomed to it.

3. His carelessness resulted in a serious mistake.

4. His ship was in danger of sinking.

5. I was afraid of hurting her feelings.

練 習 八

A. 1. According the Bible, the love of money is the root of all evil.

2. He would see that his father and mother had enough money to prevent their ever having to worry again; he would help his brothers and sisters, and some of his cousins to have a good start in life.

3. He would help many excellent charities such as the Free China Relief Association and the Kind Hearts Fund.

4. He would buy a beautiful modern house standing in its own park, with fine gardens and a swimming pool.

5. He would travel to Hong Kong, Malaysia, Singapore, Europe, and the United States.

6. He would take great delight in giving people unexpected joy.

B. 1. Apart from the question of expense, it is too late.

2. He takes great delight in painting.

3. He is kind not only to people but also to animals.

4. He exposed himself to great danger.

5. He has given away all his money.

6. His parents helped him to get a good start in life.

練 習 九

A. 1. Because when we put forth an opinion on some topic our elders often reply that we are too young to understand.

2. If the writer's father or mother is in a bad mood then the eldest child first feels its effect; he gives vent to his feelings on the next child, and so on in order of family precedence.

3. Whenever the writer's father makes a concession, the youngest is the last to receive any of its privileges.

4. Whenever a gift is presented to the family, he is the last to view it firsthand.

5. The only precedence the writer 'enjoys' is being first in the order of succession to bed.

6. In matters of amusement, our parents seem to know better than we what we enjoy.

7. In financial matters, our parents seem to think that the younger we are, the less need of money we have.

8. He mentions that children are slighted by shopkeepers, and that children are in demand for running errands and doing household chores, and for being employed in such distasteful tasks as taking the garbage out in the worst of weather.

B. 1. The more money he has, the more he spends.

2. The higher we climb, the colder the air becomes.

3. He put forth a new theory.

4. He gave vent to his anger.

5. They are prohibited from riding bicycles on the sidewalk.

6. He made no mention of this fact.

練 習 十

A. 1. If we don't have an occasional break from our daily routine, our health and our work will suffer as a result.

2. The majority travel to the seaside during the summer.

3. The more energetic people prefer to spend their holidays hiking.

4. For the inexperienced hiker easily falls victim to insect bites or foot and skin soreness, unless he wears appropriate clothing.

5. Some people prefer pitching tent in designated campsites.

6. They go sailing, mountaineering, or exploring.

7. The key to having a good time is proper planning and preparation.

B. 1. After breakfast, I brush my teeth as a matter of course.

2. The gambler fell victim to his own vice.

3. Always keep my advice in mind.

4. This doesn't meet my requirements.

5. No matter where you go, I'll be with you.

練 習 十 一

A. 1. An invention usually illustrates the truth that today's luxuries are tomorrow's necessities.

2. Inventions which are needed come easily to mind when we think of our comfort and convenience.

3. We need a machine that will not only compute figures but write compositions for us! We need a machine that will translate foreign languages and which at the push of a button will give us the answer to any question we care to ask.

4. The best inventions would be those which could cure illnesses and do away with disease.

5. We would never deceive and never be deceived. International relations would be affected. There would be no ulterior motives at council tables, and government officials on the take would all but disappear.

6. The pace of modern progress is so fast that we can safely say no invention dreamed of today is beyond the possibility of perfection tomorrow.

B. 1. She is all but seven years old.

2. He put his glasses on to read the newspaper.

3. We express our thoughts by means of words.

4. The death penalty has been done away with in many Western countries.

5. The boss doesn't think much of my work.

練 習 十 二

A. 1. It is the same today as it always has been, and it will never change. It is the most patient and cheerful of companions. It does not turn its back upon us in times of adversity or distress. It always receives us with the same kindness: amusing and instructing us in youth, and comforting and consoling us in age.

2. Because they are by far the most lasting products of human effort.

3. The only effect of time on books has been to sift out the bad products.

4. They bring us into the presence of the greatest minds that have ever lived.

5. Because preserved in books, their spirits live on.

6. Because a good book is really a rare treasure which no one should ever be without.

B. 1. Our papaya tree has grown as tall as our house.

2. Television is by far more influential than movies.

3. He turned his back on me.

4. He gave me money as well as advice.

練 習 十 三

A. 1. Stunt men are usually employed by film studios to do daring deeds which will excite movie audience.

2. The cost of life insurance for such people must be enormous, for they face accident and even death several times a day.

3. It is the thrill of living dangerously that compels them to be professional stunt men.

4. They work skillfully at dizzying heights, or put their heads in lions' mouths, or swallow a mouthful of fire. They not only do their work brilliantly but seem to enjoy every

dangerous minute of it.

5. Explorers readily admit that they enjoy the element of danger in what they do.

6. Most people probably never think about the danger of their work because it suits them better than any other activity.

7. It is probably something deep down in the human race which inspires us to conquer the unknown and to take delight in seeking adventure.

B. 1. All men thrive on freedom.

2. The lawyer could not help but disagree.

3. My father takes great delight in fishing every Sunday.

4. No matter where you want to go in the city, you can always find a taxi to take you there.

練 習 十 四

A. 1. Science has completely revolutionized the life of the average housewife.

2. The most marked developments are to be seen in the kitchen.

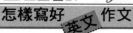

3. New scientific methods have given us stainless steel and aluminum utensils.

4. It is the manufacture of liquid detergents and cleansing powders to keep the kitchen spotless.

5. Electricity has brought the most change and given the greatest benefit to the housewife.

6. Large, comfortable bathtubs with hot running water at one's disposal make taking a bath an absolute pleasure. The ceramic industry has provided beautiful and easy-to-clean patterned tiles for both floors and walls.

7. Plastic paints in every color imaginable, or wallpaper of any design, can help to create any atmosphere desired.

8. The stereo, tape recorder, television, and radio can help the housewife to relax between chores or at the end of the day.

B. 1. She is no longer a beautiful young women.

2. The crowd kept the thief from running away.

3. We now have enough manpower at our disposal to complete the job quickly.

4. My elder sister spends a whole hour taking a bath.

練 習 十 五

A. 1. The power of the human will is immense because it is of such force that nothing can stand against it.

2. From damp caves to high-rise apartments is not a long time compared with the history of the earth, and the stride from kindling to atomic power, from a candle to an electric lamp is gigantic.

3. We can think of many people who started life without a dime and who are now millionaires; we may point to the many men and women without a formal education who are now leading executives in large corporations; we may also point to many a humble inventor whose name has become a household word—all because he was determined to find a way to reach his goal.

4. There are many people who, though not so gifted as others, have by sheer diligence surpassed their more brilliant fellows.

5. He succeeded in overthrowing the Manchu Dynasty only after suffering repeated setbacks.

6. We can reflect on the determination of the early Christians who faced death and torture to propagate their faith, of the philosophers who faced public disgrace to further their ideas —all of whom overcame immense obstacles by perseverance and an unshakeable belief in a higher goal.

B. 1. This rule holds true in every case.

2. Lincoln stood against slavery.

3. Coca Cola has become a household word even among the Chinese.

4. I was unable to improve upon his translation.

5. I couldn't think of his name at the time.

6. He set a bad example to his younger brother by wearing long hair.

練 習 十 六

A. 1. Taiwan is situated in the warm waters off the coast of mainland China.

2. Most people who visit Taiwan are amazed at the harmonious blending of the traditional and the modern.

3. In Taipei, visitors may see ornate temples and towering office buildings, high-rise apartments and tile-roofed houses, handicraft and bric-a-brac stores and ultra-modern department stores —all within a few square miles. They may see the history of the distant past in the Confucian Temple. They may also see the history of days just past in the Dr. Sun Yat-sen Memorial Hall and the Chiang Kai-shek Memorial Park.

4. Because, housing over 250,000 Chinese art treasures spanning the entire 5,000-year history of China, the museum displays only a small fraction of its collection at any one time.

5. Yeh Liu offers exciting views of the cliff, the sea, and the nearby fishing villages and beaches. It is a unique and frequently visited spot because of its reddish coral rock formations.

6. Some scenic spots in central Taiwan are Mt. Ali, Sun Moon Lake, Pao Chueh Temple, and the Taroko Gorge.

7. In southern Taiwan, the visitor shouldn't miss the Kenting Tropical Park.

8. Because the Chinese have been called the politest and friendliest people on earth, and nowhere else in the world can traditional Chinese culture be experienced by the

foreigner than on this bastion of freedom.

B. 1. The river abounds with fish.

2. I don't have anything in particular to do tomorrow.

3. She wrote a poem in memory of her grandmother.

4. I fell in love with my new neighbor the moment I set eyes on her.

練 習 十 七

A. 1. Few people surely have failed to notice at some time or other a little green van speeding through the streets, or a young man dressed in green pedaling down a lane on his bicycle, or a pair of mailboxes along the roadside.

2. Apart from ordinary correspondence, the post office handles a steady stream of bulk mail, the vast rush of the Christmas greeting cards, thousands of parcels and packages of various sizes, and a very large volume of domestic and foreign periodicals. It also handles the register and express services, the surface mail and air mail to every free nation in the world.

3. We may safely mail money to anyone in Taiwan by using a postal money order. We may use the postal remittance service to buy the latest publications or the newest gadgets. We can deposit money there. The post office also accepts payment of utility bills.

4. The topics of such stamps are paintings and masterpieces of calligraphy, bronze, ceramics, jade, and tapestry found in the collection of the National Palace Museum.

5. Since its establishment in 1896, the Chinese Post Office has steadily grown in size and in importance.

B. 1. He never thinks of anyone but himself.

2. Mary was so careless as to forget to bring her book.

3. There is little doubt that we will win.

4. There is little time left.

5. Don't hurry, you still have a little time.

6. Few people know it.

7. A few people know it.

練 習 十 八

A. 1. She heartily congratulates Sue because Sue had passed her examination.

2. Sue's elder brother should have some exciting stories to tell when he comes home on leave.

3. Lilly is going to be a secretary.

4. She saw a special exhibition of Sung Dynasty paintings.

5. She tries to get a better understanding of American humor.

6. Because that book is a good introduction to Chinese life and culture.

7. Mary went shopping downtown last Saturday with her mother to have a dress made for herself.

8. She has been going to shadow-boxing classes every morning.

9. Paul and Mary went to the movies together last Sunday. From this Sue can gather that their relationship is progressing.

B. 1. I am looking for my pen.

2. The children are looking forward to the holidays.

3. He went back to the United States on leave.

4. They made fun of him behind his back.

5. He had a pair of leather boots made for NT$1000.

練 習 十 九

A. 1. The television announced that super typhoon Betty had unexpectedly changed course.

2. His mother filled the bathtub with water. His elder sister went to the neighborhood grocery store to purchase some nonperishables, such as noodles and canned goods. His father collected the potted plants stored them in the small, enclosed back porch. He also and climbed a bamboo ladder and took down the TV antenna. The writer was responsible for preparing the necessary candles and making sure that the flashlight had fresh batteries.

3. The full fury of the storm hit while the writer's family were enjoying their dinner.

4. He turned on the flashlight; then he got up to light the candles.

5. They all seated themselves once again at the dinner table to finish their meal.

6. A white mass of matted fur darted into the living room. Poor, frightened Whitey ran under the sofa and stayed there for the duration of the storm.

7. A resounding thud echoed through the house.

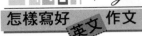
8. Each family member rushed to a different window to see what had happened.

9. The papaya tree had fallen directly on Whitey's doghouse, smashing it to pieces.

B. 1. There were at least thirty people there.

2. I will get up at six o'clock tomorrow.

3. Please turn the television on so that I may watch the news.

4. We should take precautions against accidents.

5. The thief broke into our house while we were away.

6. He spent all afternoon waiting for her phone call, only to discover that his phone was out of order.

練 習 二 十

A. 1. He was born in a middle-class neighborhood in Taipei.

2. As the eldest child, the writer had always had the responsibility of looking after his little brothers and sisters when their patents were elsewhere occupied.

3. His father is the manager of a trading company and often travels, both to southern Taiwan and to other countries in Asia.

4. His mother is a housewife. She often takes on odd jobs like sewing garments for his uncle when his tailor shop gets too busy, or helps to cook meals at his aunt's small restaurant whenever she becomes short-handed.

5. He consistently received the highest grades in his class in arithmetic.

6. He started to develop a keen interest in reading.

7. He began to devote more and more of his spare time to developing his English language ability. He read simplified editions of Western classics, listened to radio plays on ICRT, and watched English language movies and TV programs.

8. Upon graduation, his parents surprised him with a set of annotated English readers and cassette tapes as a present.

9. His English has been improving by leaps and bounds.

10. He has dreams of becoming a great writer and translator.

B. 1. He is living with his cousin for the time being.

2. Will you look after my garden while I'm away?

3. To the best of my memory, her birthday is tomorrow.

4. He took on the responsibility of caring for the orphan.

5. The population is growing by leaps and bounds.

練 習 二 十 一

A. 1. His electric alarm clock goes off each school day morning at 6:15.

2. He gropes his way to the bathroom to wash up.

3. He seats himself in front of a bowl of steaming congee and a dish of dried meat floss.

4. Halfway through breakfast he glances at his watch: as usual it reads 6:40.

5. Sprinting is not only good exercise but also very invigorating first thing in the morning.

6. A morning does not pass without his being squeezed into a motorized can, without an elbow being jabbed in his ribs, and without his brightly polished shoes being stepped on and dirtied.

7. He usually spends this time glancing over his lessons.

8. He goes to the athletic field for an exciting game of basketball or soccer.

9. After dinner, he relaxes in the living room and enjoys some fruit while watching the evening news. Then he withdraws to the quiet of his room after the news and bury himself in his schoolwork.

10. Before retiring, he wishes his parents good night, brushes his teeth, and sets his alarm clock for another routine day.

B. 1. Please turn off the light.

2. We got on the train at Taipei and got off at Taichung.

3. No matter where he tries to hide, the police will find him.

4. He buried himself in his work.

5. If you continue to work overtime every night, you will end up in a hospital.

6. He cannot speak English without making mistakes.

7. Glance over the test before answering any questions.

練 習 二 十 二

A. 1. It was one of learning by doing.

2. They arrived at their lake-side campsite at 11:00 on a crisp autumn morning.

3. They stood by the edge of the lake drinking in the changing fall colors and isolated silence.

4. Because the lake was beckoning them to refresh their worn-out bodies in its soothing water.

5. They began to make plans for setting up camp.

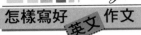

6. After lunch, they chopped sufficient fuel to last through the night, and hunted around the forest for some wild fruit and berries.

7. They knew it from the buzzing of mosquitoes.

8. During dinner, they decided to rough it the first night: they would sleep in the open air in their sleeping bags.

9. After dinner, they cleaned up their campsite, washed the pot, and tied their trash in a plastic bag.

10. Around midnight, a snorting sound woke them up. They realized the snorting-like sounds were coming from an animal searching through their trash for a midnight snack. It was a small bear.

11. They decided that they would procrastinate no longer: even before cleaning up the mess, they would set up their tent.

B. 1. She cleaned up the house for her tea party.

2. He changed into his work clothes.

3. We camped out for a week.

4. They set up a stand by the roadside and sold fruit.

5. Please wake me up at five.

練 習 二 十 三

A.　1.　He had always wanted to meet a film star, especially one of the great martial arts actors of the Bruce Lee type.

2.　Because they wanted to enjoy some of the things which were impractical to do in a large group.

3.　They had decided to take a trip in a motorboat to an island a short distance away.

4.　They passed the time building sandcastles and digging for sand crabs.

5.　They were dressed in light T-shirts and jeans.

6.　As they neared the island they suddenly saw a beautiful yacht anchored in a hidden cove.

7.　As they approached the yacht, a bearded foreigner appeared and invited them to spend the day on the yacht.

8.　Their delight turned into rapture when they learned they were in the company of Jackie Chan and Chuck Norris, the two world-famous kung fu actors.

9.　They were on location filming scenes for their upcoming American-made movie.

10.　They didn't appear to be playacting, for they were exchanging real blow for real blow.

11. After lunch, they sunbathed on the deck of the yacht, listening to Jackie and Chuck reminisce about their acting experiences.

B. 1. He has gone without his dinner, and yet he goes on with his work.

2. He pitted his endurance against the other man's speed.

3. The manager showed us around the factory.

4. The housekeeper agreed to stay on until a replacement could be found.

5. My best friend and I reminisced about our childhood days.

練 習 二 十 四

A. 1. On the positive side, television is a vast encyclopedia of knowledge.

2. Television can also serve to stimulate the fertile imagination of the young.

3. Television is used by many parents as a nursemaid or as a babysitter for a restless or cranky child; and more often than not, it is the violent cartoons or morally questionable soap operas that produce the calming effect.

4. Fast-paced TV programs are more like a "wolf in sheep's clothing", for they have made the young less patient.

5. Along with its benefits, television has brought enormous problems.

B. 1. He works hard in order to keep his family in comfort.

2. We succeeded in spite of all difficulties.

3. I am accustomed to this sort of work.

4. In order that every student might understand it, the teacher explained that passage again and again.

5. Can you do the work on your own?

6. Chinese parents exercise great influence over their children.

練 習 二 十 五

A. 1. He agrees only partly with the common saying that the best things in life are free.

2. There is nothing more exhilarating than a beautiful sunset with colorful clouds drifting across the sky, or than some awe-inspiring form such as a lofty mountain or a stormy sea. The natural elements in their varying forms give us a kind of free entertainment which nothing can surpass.

3. One of the best things in life is undeniably free: friendship.

4. Enjoyment of artistic things also free.

5. It requires a large bank balance.

6. We must first have a high-paying job to be able to afford gas and maintenance.

7. One of the finest things we can ever enjoy is the achievement of our ambitions.

8. The least costly and most rewarding attainment is that of spiritual peace.

B. 1. How do you get around in the city? By bus?

2. He agreed to the terms of payment.

3. I agreed with you in your views.

4. He is not to be relied on.

5. He ate to his heart's content, and got a stomachache afterwards.

6. No matter what he says, it makes no difference to me.

7. There's nothing better for a cold than rest.

大地 Learning 叢書介紹

怎樣寫好英文作文—基礎入門篇

主編：吳奚真
合編：張先信、Phillip Podgur
定價：180元

英文教學要培養四種基本能力：聽的能力、閱讀的能力、口頭表達能力、和文字表達能力。英文作文屬於文字能力的表達，就文字能力的表達而言，最根本的辦法當然是從培養語言習慣做起，很自然的養成基本的表達能力，對於中學生而言，這種能力的培養有賴於有意的「記憶」和「模仿」。本書針對中學生在學習英文作文方面，提供了一套完整的學習模式，從句子的形式、基本句形，句子的組合……由淺入深，循序漸進。書中各章並附有練習，熟讀本書必能讓你在英文作文的學習方面達到良好的效果。

大地 Learning 叢書介紹

英語散文集錦

編譯：吳奚真

定價：170元

本書選擇精簡散文29篇。部份選自吳教授在師大講授英國散文之教材，或由其翻譯之書籍中摘出。原文與譯文均極優美，並對立身處世之道有啟發，為自修英文與增進修養之最佳讀物

國家圖書館出版品預行編目資料

怎樣寫好英文作文. 應用進階篇／張先信，
　Phillip Podgur 編著. -- 一版. -- 臺北
市：大地，2003〔民92〕
　　面；　公分-- （Learning；7）

　　ISBN 957-8290-77-2（平裝）
　　1. 英國語言－作文－教學法　2. 中等教育
524.383　　　　　　　　　　92002599

Learning 07

怎樣寫好英文作文・應用進階篇

編　　著：張先信，Phillip Podgur

主　　編：吳奚眞

創 辦 人：姚宜瑛

發 行 人：吳錫清

美術編輯：普林特斯資訊有限公司

出 版 者：大地出版社

社址：台北市內湖區瑞光路358巷38弄36號4樓之2

劃撥帳號：50031946（戶名：大地出版社有限公司）

電　　話：(02)2627－7749

傳　　真：(02)2627－0895

E-mail：vastplai@ms45.hinet.net

印 刷 者：普林特斯資訊股份有限公司

一版四刷：2012年3月

定　　價：220元